GW00569720

Getting the
Buddha Mind

master sheng-yen

Acknowledgments

Editor	Ernest Heau
Editorial Assistance (First Printing)	Harry Miller Dan Stevenson Karen Swaine
Editorial Assistance (Second Printing)	Harry Miller Nancy Patchen
Translators	Ming-Yee Wang Paul Kennedy Karen Swaine
Transcriber	Karen Swaine
Book Design	Trish Ing
Cover Design	Page Simon
Cover Photographer	Lili Lauritano
Back Photographer	Ching-lung Chen

Dharma Drum Publications is the publishing activity of

Institute of Chung-Hwa Buddhist Culture
90-56 Corona Avenue
Elmhurst, New York 11373

Library of Congress Catalog Card Number 82-73979
ISBN 0-9609854-0-9

Contents

Author's Preface

I arrived in America in the winter of 1975 to present the teaching and the experience of Ch'an Buddhism. Though I have written in both Chinese and Japanese I cannot express myself as well in English. In this respect, I may have failed to fulfill some expectations that people had of me.

Fortunately, among my American disciples and students, are several who have a good command of both English and Chinese. Thus, when I speak of Ch'an teaching and practice, my remarks are translated immediately into English. On formal occasions, such as retreats, lectures, and seminars, these remarks are also taped. Many of these talks, after transcription, organization, and editing, are published in two of our publications, *Ch'an Magazine* and *Ch'an Newsletter*. Many readers have expressed interest in and appreciation for these articles, thus providing the first causing-condition for publishing this book.

Ch'an is the supreme realization of the original nature of mind. It neither affirms nor negates any conceptual point of view, hence does not need language for its expression. On the other hand, one can exhaust the resources of language, and still not express the ultimate Ch'an. This is because Ch'an transcends knowledge, symbols, and all the apparatus of language.

You may call Ch'an "emptiness," but it is not emptiness in the nihilistic sense of "there's nothing there." You may call it "existence," but it is not existence in the common sense of "I see it, so it must be there." It is existence which transcends the fictions of our sense impressions of the world, of sight, sound, smell, taste, touch, and form. Yet this Ch'an is never apart from our everyday world. It is indwelling in all beings, everywhere, at all times.

This Ch'an is none other than our original self, which has been hidden from view since time unremembered by our egocentric delusions. In Ch'an Buddhism this self is called by various terms, such as the "pure mind of self-nature," or "Buddha-nature." It is the self which has been liberated from egocentrism. As such, it is coextensive with space and time, yet not limited by such concepts. It is pure wisdom; it is transcendent, absolute freedom.

The path by which this self is revealed and experienced is the path of Ch'an, and its methods of practice. Itself beyond description, Ch'an uses language as a bridge, until practitioners can themselves enter the door of Ch'an. This is the second causing-condition for this book.

Since being in America, I have spoken on many aspects of Ch'an practice, and many students have found these talks beneficial to their practice. Among these were talks in a special category, which some of my senior students felt should be collected into a book. These talks pertain to the practice of the seven-day Ch'an retreat, and in fact, were mainly given on such retreats over the past five years. The distinctive mark of these talks is that they are guides to practice, and have only incidental interest in theory or doctrine.

The goal of the Ch'an retreat is the furtherance of practice, and when the causes and conditions are ripe, the actual experience of Ch'an – of "seeing self-nature," or "getting the Buddha-mind." In one way or another, all the talks point in the direction of guiding and helping students along the path of liberation. The retreats are occasions for energetically practicing together; the talks, signposts along the way. I hope that their publication can bring some insight and help to the growing number of Americans who find benefit in the study and practice of Buddhism. This is the third and final causing-condition for this book.

The preparation of this book has been a collaboration by several people, over a span of time, beginning with on-the-spot translations, primarily by Ming-Yee Wang. Other translators include Paul Kennedy and Karen Swaine. Transcription, typing, and collection of the texts was done mostly by Karen

Swaine. Marina Heau proofread the manuscript. Nancy Makso coordinated the printing effort. Rick Halsted proofread the printer's galleys. Organization and editing of the text was done by Ernest Heau, with the assitance of Karen Swaine, Harry Miller, and Dan Stevenson. Bringing the whole book together as chief editor, Ernest Heau has dedicated the most energy of all. I hereby express my thanks to these individuals.

Ch'an Master Sheng-yen
Ch'an Meditation Center
Elmhurst, New York
July 15, 1982

Editor's Introduction

I. THE CH'AN RETREAT

Clack! Clack! Clack!
Clack! Clack! Clack!

Dawn breaks hard on the sleepy practitioner. It is 4:15 A.M. and the clapping of the morning boards signals another day of retreat. "Is it already four hours since I eased my aching body — this figment of my mind — into the sleeping bag? Will I make it through another day? I? I? But who am I? To whom does this sleepiness and confusion belong? Better get up. Bathroom will be busy. Shih-fu didn't seem pleased with me yesterday. Must pull myself together today!"

This avalanche of mindstuff, though imaginary, typifies a kind of mental state that grips many a practitioner, especially during the early days of a Ch'an seven-day retreat. It is a mind confused, and distracted by pain and suffering, but basically not unlike the mental states experienced daily by the average person. It is a state of preoccupation with one's private predicament, ruled by an army of doubts.

The difference is that the self-confrontation of the retreat brings into focus the distractions of an entire lifetime; indeed, in the teachings of Buddhism, the accumulated delusions of eons of rebirth. What is the source of these delusions? On a superficial level, it is the belief in the overriding importance of one's private predicament. This is no great revelation. All the great ethical and religious systems address the question of self and selfishness in one way or another.

But the unique spirit of Buddhism is to challenge the fervent belief in the reality of that predicament itself, especially its private nature. Buddhism does not deny existence, or that existence is problematic. The central teaching is that the belief in a private predicament, a focus of interests and attitudes called the self, is itself the seeding ground of the problems of existence.

Master Sheng-yen tells us, "Where there is a body, there is vexation." Recognizing this poignant truth would lead one straightaway to the path of practice, if one's sense of bodily existence were keen enough. Practice to escape having a body? Of course not. Practice to learn that the possession of a body need not lead unalterably to delusion, minute after minute, day after day, life after life; practice to begin unravelling the threads of karma that knot us to our yearnings.

It is the phenomenon of having a body with sense faculties that is the root cause of vexation. And what is vexation? It is pain and suffering, but it is also pleasure and joy. At its most subtle level, vexation accompanies any change in the mind/body state, for it is the nature of the organism to avoid pain and adversity, and to prolong pleasure and comfort. As phenomena, our bodies undergo change constantly, so that subliminal as well as overt vexation are constant facts of life. Disease, unhappiness, and death may sometimes seem to come as chance events, but in reality are climaxes to hidden dramas long in the making. We are vexed even as we remain ignorant of vexation.

While the mind/body aggregate leads to a notion of self, and all the consequences that flow from that, it also contains all the possibilities of awakening to the Buddha mind, the true self-nature. "You must start with grasping the narrow sense of self. You must know this self in a very clear and solid manner." So says Master Sheng-yen to those starting on the path of practice. And again, "The self is not to be despised; it is your vehicle to selflessness."

This pragmatic recognition of the need to start at some graspable level of certainty typifies the method of Master Sheng-yen, and that of his spiritual lineage, Ch'an Buddhism. At the same time, the method of Ch'an deliberately cultivates in its practitioners a driving sense of urgency. This radical earnestness of Ch'an is exemplified in the account that the First Partriarch of Ch'an, the Indian Bodhidharma, sat in meditation for nine years facing a blank wall.

Still, it would be a mistake to confuse this earnestness with asceticism or fanaticism. (The austere and zealous style of Ch'an is balanced by a gentle tolerance of human frailty, and an exquisite wit.) The intensity of Ch'an is a product of a precise method, animated by a deep faith in the example and the teaching of Sakyamuni, the Buddha of the current epoch. Again, it would be a mistake to make a mechanistic interpretation of the precision of Ch'an, and practitioners without a qualified master may fall into this error.

The paradigm of Ch'an, that which most reveals its intensity, precision, and spiritual ardor, is the relationship between master and disciple. The intensity is the result of the dynamic interplay between master and disciple in a game having the highest stakes: the eventual enlightenment of the disciple. This is crucial in a retreat because the disciple's presence there is a signal that he accepts the master's guidance. By coming to retreat, the student also accepts the challenge, unmistakably defined by the master, of bringing to bear all his physical and mental resources to progress to spiritual awakening. From the moment retreat begins, to the moment it ends, the relationship of both master and student is defined by this understanding. To go on retreat with notions less rigorous than this is to start with an extra burden.

The relationship of master and disciple may be likened to that of patient and doctor. That the patient is ill is not in dispute. The illness is the patient's inability to abandon the delusions he has been harboring since birth. This inability is ultimately due to a deeply imbedded craving for form and existence, a desire for experience, carried as a karmic burden from one life to the next. Form and existence, when coupled with sentient faculties, lead eventually to the invention of a new and very sophisticated form, the self or "I". If left unrestrained, the "I" soon becomes the overlord of our conscious life. The belief in the self-entity is the root delusion which proliferates new delusions without end, and seemingly without regard to their consequences. If health means abandoning the habits of falling into delusion, then a radical re-education towards the idea of I/self is needed. The course of cure begins with the patient's recognition of his state, and his submission to the ministrations of his doctor, the Ch'an master.

The single most important qualification of the Ch'an master is that he has himself completed the same course of cure under his own master. In this sense he is not like the cancer specialist who has never had cancer, or the psychiatrist who has never been psychotic. He has himself traveled the path out of delusion on which he now guides his students. Beyond that, his level of attainment, his style, energy, eloquence, the qualities of his master, are individual matters. In any case, the significance of this qualification has to do with the notion of transmission.

Master Sheng-yen says, "Transmission means that the student has had a Buddha-mind experience and the experience was recognized by a master." On one level, the transmission certifies the student's achievement; on another level, it certifies the method and lineage of Ch'an masters; on the highest level, it certifies the way and teaching of the Buddha.

What is the significance of the Buddha-mind experience? At a low level, it means that the practitioner has at least momentarily broken through the wall of delusion that prevented him from seeing his original nature, which is that of a Buddha. He discovers that this wall is really the old habitual ways of thinking and acting, which have been gradually eroded by patient and rigorous practice and meditation under a master. At a high level, it means that the disciple has become enlightened. At any level, it is only a beginning, for the path is without limits.

From the moment retreat begins, the zealous practitioner will make a determined effort to gain the Buddha-mind experience. To aim lower would be disrespectful to his master and a disservice to himself. Yet, the conscious evocation of such a goal is fraught with problems, and may become an enormous distraction. It has been said that to travel the spiritual path is to walk on the edge of a razor. On one side, the disciple may fall into indifference and indolence, on the other, into frustration and despair. The student must develop and maintain an exquisite balance, a concentrated detachment, to stay on course and make progress.

In most cases, and certainly with beginners, this is impossible without the strict guidance and intimate involvement of the Ch'an master. To bring students to a plane of consistent and productive effort, the master applies the meditative methods of Ch'an to help them cut off their clinging to private concerns, to settle their minds, as a precondition for an awakening. Master Sheng-yen says, "When the mind is settled, it opens up."

When the student's mind becomes calm and concentrated, it can be further refined and concentrated until it reaches a deep state of absorption, or samadhi. From there, one can make progress towards the experience of awakening.

In Master Sheng-yen's words, we "start with the scattered mind, bring it to samadhi, and using the method of Ch'an, dissolve the unified state. The scattered mind lacks focus and energy. The student's energy must be collected and concentrated." This statement suggests that besides being spiritual guide and meditation teacher, the Ch'an master is also a psychologist who must be very perceptive about the mental states of his students. Because it is not possible to achieve such intimate rapport with a large group, Master Sheng-yen limits his retreats to a small number of participants.

The spiritual ardor of Ch'an is faith in action. It arises out of a state of mind based on a collaboration between master and disciple. The energy source from which both draw is their faith in the teaching and method transmitted from Sakyamuni, down through the patriarchs and masters. The state of mind that is created is one in which the conditions exist to allow, in Master Sheng-yen's words, "a cataclysmic experience" to happen.

For most students, the only context in which this can happen is the Ch'an retreat. While the retreat experience is a matter of individual effort and interaction with the master, it is also a profoundly shared collective experience. As participants settle into the practice and surrender their private outlook, the boundaries of their sense of identification gradually soften, and in so doing, widen. The retreat routine dictates that everybody does the same thing at the same time, foregoing distractions such as conversation and socializing. The schedule is filled with meditation, interviews with the master, preparing meals, working, reciting morning, afternoon, and evening services, and hearing Dharma talks by the master. There is no surplus time for pursuing private interests. Even time in the bathroom is minimal because of the limited accomodations. Finally, there are frequent reminders from the master to maintain the practice even during rest periods after meals.

All this has a powerful effect on mood and feeling. There is a collective mind from which all draw strength and encouragement. While struggling with their private drama, all find in this common well some comfort and energy to help them move forward. Setting the tone and tempo, is the Ch'an master. His words, actions, gestures, even silence, provide the focus and the motivating energy. To those who have stilled their minds and attained deep concentration, there may come feelings of great peace, exhilaration, bliss, and awe. Their samadhi and composure in turn affect the others, lifting all to higher dedication.

However, such feelings may become distractions, ends in themselves, easily mistaken as genuine realization. Now, the Ch'an master's work becomes one of midwifery. He must guide and inspire the student, whose mind has ripened, to the more arduous effort that will be needed to give birth to the Buddha-mind. Before this can happen, the student must develop "a great ball of doubt." Master Sheng-yen says, "Getting the Buddha-mind depends on developing a great ball of doubt which drives the student to energetic and diligent practice. This is not the everyday kind of doubt, but doubt that comes from great faith and determination." The Ch'an master's skill is most revealed in how he brings the student to this state, how he causes the "ball of doubt" to grow in the student's mind. While we call this "skill," it is actually a spontaneous expression of the master's compassion, which is not a sentiment, but a function of wisdom.

When the disciple's response to the master's compassion is intense spiritual ardor, or faith, this allows the "doubt mass" to gather great energy. The conditions being right, ultimately there may come a sense of surrender. When the sense of surrender reaches the extreme, when seeking, clinging, and conceptualizing are left behind, the mind is free to open. When the mind opens, the disciple crosses a threshold and enters "the door of Ch'an." This cataclysmic experience is *wu*, or "emptiness." It is seeing self-nature; it is getting the Buddha-mind.

II. THE BOOK

The present book consists primarily of lectures given by Master Sheng-yen at Ch'an retreats in America between 1975 and 1980. As such, they do not form a structured whole in the sense of presenting a theoretical view of Ch'an Buddhism. Far from it. As a scholar of Chinese Buddhism, Master Sheng-yen does have some interest in theory, and his other books bear that out. As a teacher of meditation, however, Master Sheng-yen is rooted in the practical. The lectures are given by Master Sheng-yen to instruct, encourage, inspire, even cajole and caution, but never to "educate."

To the extent these lectures form a whole, it is because they rise out of a consistent and informed approach to teaching Ch'an meditation. The Ch'an retreat is chosen as a model because it brings together the many historical threads of the Ch'an tradition. It is in fact the living demonstration of the idea of "transmission of mind without the use of words," espoused by Bodhidharma in the sixth century A.D.

The book begins with a brief autobiography of Master Sheng-yen, followed by the chapter of "The Ch'an Seven Day Retreat." Both of these were lectures given at the editor's request, to provide background for the book. The chapter on "Four Conditions For Practicing Ch'an" is actually an expansion of a previous retreat lecture, again, provided at the editor's request. All the other lectures are based on tape-recorded transcripts of retreat lectures.

The major part of the book then consists of selections from among many lectures. The purpose was to present a broad picture of Master Sheng-yen's methodology of meditation, and his explanation of the experience of enlightenment. The emphasis was to focus on the practice of meditation, and on guidelines for making progress.

Two long chapters, "On Silent Illumination" and "On Contemplating Mind," are based on commentaries of poems by two famous Ch'an Masters, Hung-Chih, and Han-Shan. The poems are didactic and are addressed to advanced practitioners. Master Sheng-yen uses the poems as points of departure for his own commentary, which has its own focus in the actual retreat setting.

As presented, the talks are the end result of translation, transcription, and editing. Inevitably, this filtering results in some loss of the original flavor of Master Sheng-yen's language and delivery. However, the translators and editors have strived to preserve the original sense and meaning of Master Sheng-yen's words. To the extent that this goal has not been achieved, the fault lies with the coordinating editor.

Part Three of the book contains several accounts of retreat experiences of disciples and students of Master Sheng-yen. These accounts are presented because they convey interesting and, hopefully, useful insights into the retreat process from the student's point of view. The students range from intermediate to advanced in meditation experience. The accounts are not offered as models of aspiration. Every Ch'an student brings to the retreat a unique set of attitudes and responses, and is therefore likely to experience something unique. Probably none of the writers would describe their experience as particularly deep. However, in each case, the experience has a certain validity, and at least hint at the possibilities. In age, they range from early twenties to early thirties; in gender, they are roughly balanced between male and female.

The experience of Ch'an is a step along the path; it is not necessarily enlightenment, and certainly not a final resting place. Master Sheng-yen tells us that there are many levels of enlightenment, and that the ultimate enlightenment is to finally transcend enlightenment, and to dwell in pure existence. Even so, to experience Ch'an is a necessary step to enlightenment. Master Sheng-yen says, "To get the Buddhamind and to be confirmed are strong reasons for attending retreats."

Part Four consists of the transcription of a radio interview with Mr. Lex Hixon on Station WBAI in New York City. This interview is included because of the insights it gives to Master Sheng-yen's method for conducting retreats.

To call this book a collection of retreat lectures by Master Sheng-yen is to call a pile of dead leaves a tree. Abstracted from the somber, intense, and frequently very moving context of the Ch'an retreat, these reproductions have already lost much of their immediacy. Every day, after the evening meal, comes a brief rest period. The practitioners meditate, sit, or stand about, waiting for Master Sheng-yen to enter for the evening lecture.

There is no conversation. It has been a hard day for all. Up since 4:15 A.M., all have gone through the same rigorous schedule, including a total of about eight hours of sitting meditation. Their mental and physical states vary. Some are distracted and discouraged by the pain and strain of long sitting. Others have transcended their physical problems and have settled their minds enough to begin experiencing deeper meditative states. All are bonded in a common undertaking – to practice Ch'an.

To some this means spiritual realization; to others, perhaps a way to improve their emotional lives or health. These distinctions do not matter to Master Sheng-yen. He speaks to all as fellow travelers on the path. When Master Sheng-yen enters to give his talk, the mood is already palpable with a feeling that can be described as reverence. This reverence, although personified in Master Sheng-yen, actually transcends his person. This is no accident, for it is Master Sheng-yen himself who imbues his students with a profound sense of the teaching of the Buddha, and an example of the Bodhisattvas. This mood is all the more poignant for being devoid of any sense of worship; the Buddha is perceived as a teacher and exemplar, not a god.

Though frail of body, Master Sheng-yen conveys a sense of great spiritual energy. From morning till night, his presence dominates and sets the tone; the mental climate of the retreat is the collective mind of all present, but it is also shaped and guided by the master's personality. To experience Master Sheng-yen's rebuke is to be truly humbled; to receive his compassion is to be moved to tears. He is also a very funny man, capable of hilarious feats of story-telling and mimicry. When delivering the lessons of the Dharma, his dark eyes blaze with zeal, so that even the English translation which follows can become superflous. When he comforts a suffering student in front of everyone, all are comforted.

These are the things that are lost in these printed pages. Even so, to one who has never seen a tree, even dead leaves may contain a lesson about the nature of trees. To those who have never experienced a Ch'an retreat, this book may hopefully convey something of the method, the intent, and the flavor of this unique form of spiritual training. If this happens to any degree, the publishers will feel less ashamed for having offered to the reader a pile of dead leaves.

Ernest Heau
New York City
November 1982

PART
ONE

Introduction to Ch'an

Autobiography

I was born on a farm in the countryside near Shanghai. At the age of thirteen I left home to become a
Buddhist monk. The local monastery I entered, like
most others in China, was called a Ch'an temple. But,
in fact the theory and practice of Ch'an was almost
never discussed there. As young monks, most of us
did not have any clear idea of what Ch'an practice
really was. Our training simply consisted of the
rigorous discipline prescribed for monks – everyday
activities such as washing clothes, working in the
fields, cooking and performing daily services. We also
studied major sutras such as the Amitabha, the Lotus,
and the Diamond Sutras. Daily chores, however,
were not a problem for me; the worst thing was
memorizing sutras. There were so many to learn, and
I felt very stupid. My master told me, "Your karmic
obstructions are very heavy. You should make a
strong effort to atone for them. Go prostrate to Kuan
Yin Bodhisattva."

There was little time for practice during the day,
so I prostrated to Kuan Yin five hundred times at

night, and again before the morning boards. After doing this for three months, I was overcome one day with a very refreshed and comfortable feeling. It seemed as if the whole world had changed. My mind became very clear and very bright. Memorization was no longer a problem, and I began to learn very quickly. To this day I believe Kuan Yin gave me assistance. Most important, there arose in me a deep sense of responsiblility towards the Dharma.

I was thirteen years old and knew nothing about the history of Buddhism, yet I felt that Buddhism was on the way to extinction. Most Chinese had little understanding of the Dharma. Teachers were very rare, and what I knew came only from memorizing the scriptures. Chinese Buddhism did not provide a systematic education for monks. A monk's training was usually completed gradually and imperceptibly through the experience of everyday life. There simply was no planned education. I felt sympathy for those who had never heard the Dharma, and realized the importance of reviving Buddhism. I vowed to learn more about the Buddha Dharma so that one day I might bring it to others.

Because of Communist opposition in the area, our monks moved to Shanghai. There our livelihood depended solely on donations from performing services for the dead. It was depressing to see monks and nuns performing perfunctory rituals instead of teaching Buddhism. I did this for two years. Through all this period, I felt that my karmic obstructions were severe. About this time, however, I learned of a seminary in Shanghai where young monks could acquire a Buddhist education. So I ran away from my monastery to study at this school. When he later arrived in Shanghai, my master approved of my decision.

At the school some people had a noble sense of purpose, but others were simply there to get an education. The seminary was founded by a student of Master T'ai-Hsu, one of the great revivers of modern Chinese Buddhism. T'ai-Hsu was in turn greatly influenced by Great Master Ou-I, of the Ming dynasty. Ou-I disapproved of sectarianism and insisted that since Sakyamuni Buddha there had been just one Buddhist tradition. He placed equal emphasis on the eight schools: Hua-yen, T'ien-t'ai, Ch'an (Zen), Wei-shih (Consciousness-only), Vinaya, Chung-kuan (Madhyamika), Ching-tu (Pure Land), and Esoteric Buddhism. At the seminary, most of the teachers were students of T'ai-Hsu.

I studied Buddhist history and the teachings of Vinaya, Wei-shih, T'ien-t'ai, and Hua-yen. The seminary also emphasized physical exercise. We learned T'ai Chi Ch'uan and Shao-lin boxing, this later from a teacher from the Shao-lin monastery. In our practice there was particular emphasis on ritual repentance. We meditated, but did not have a very clear idea of the correct method of practice. Thus it was difficult to gain any real strength from it. We supposed that it would take years to achieve benefits.

I recalled that even Sakyamuni Buddha practiced for six years. I also recalled that Master Hsu-Yun, who left home at the age of twenty, was still practicing at fifty, though the world had not yet heard of him.

People who had deep meditation experiences, or who had been certified as enlightened, never explained their experience. When they talked among themselves, their language was strange, and its meaning elusive. There were a few older students who had spent several years in meditation halls. When I asked them about practice they would say, "Oh, it's easy. Just sit there. Once your legs stop hurting it's fine." Sometimes a monk would be given a kung-an (koan) on which to meditate, but on the whole, there was no systematic meditation training.

Once at the seminary, I participated in a Ch'an retreat. I would just sit in meditation until I heard the incense board signaling walking meditation. No one told me what to do or gave me any instruction. We had a saying that one had to sit until "the bottom falls out of the barrel of pitch." Only then could he get to see the master.

Sometimes, while sitting, I thought, "What should I be doing? Should I be reciting Buddha's name? Should I be doing something else? What really is meditation?" I kept asking myself these questions until I became a big ball of doubt. However, while at this seminary, my doubts never got resolved.

Eventually, I left mainland China for Taiwan, where I was conscripted into army service. Despite my duties as a soldier, I took time to meditate everyday. My doubts, still unresolved, caused all kinds of questions to come up. There were may contradictions in the Buddhist teachings that I could not resolve. This was very disturbing since I had deep faith in the Buddha's teachings and believed that the sutras could not be wrong. I was burdened with such questions as "What is enlightenment?" "What is Buddhahood?" Questions like these filled in my mind, and I desperately needed to know the answers.

This underlying doubt was always there. When I was working it would disappear, but when I practiced, this suffocating doubt would often return. This situation persisted for years, until I was twenty-eight, when I met my first real master. I was visiting a monastery in southern Taiwan, where I sometimes lectured. I learned that a famous monk, Ling-Yuan, was also visiting. That night we happened to share the same sleeping platform. Seeing that he was meditating instead of sleeping, I sat with him. I was still burdened by my questions and was desperate to have them resolved. He seemed to be quite at ease, with no problems in the world, so I decided to approach him.

He listened patiently as I spoke of my many doubts and problems. In reply, he would just ask, "Anymore?" I contined like this for two or three hours, I was extremely agitated and anxious for answers. Finally he sighed and said, "Put down!" These words struck me like lightning. My body poured sweat, I felt like I had been instantly cured of a bad cold. I felt a great weight suddenly lift from me. It was a very comfortable and soothing feeling. We just sat there, not speaking a word. I was extremely happy. It was one of the most pleasant nights of my life. The next day I continued to experience great happiness. The whole world was fresh, as though I was seeing it for the first time.

At this time I realized two important points necessary for practice. The first has to do with "causes and conditions." Certain things not entirely under your control — your own karma, the karma of others, environmental factors — must come together in a way that favors making progress in this lifetime. To make great progress in practice you must have this karmic affinity — the proper conditions must exist.

Second, one must have effective methods of practicing under the guidance of a qualified master. From the time I left home I spent fifteen years in my practice. I thought this was much too long. In the past whenever I asked my teachers for guidance, they would just say, "Work hard. What else is there to talk about?" But now I realized there were two requirements — working hard on a good method and having a good master.

From then on I searched especially in the sutras for techniques of practice to cultivate *dhyana*. With some experience a student can usually produce results with these methods. Even though the texts are not always clear, persistence and hard work eventually bring success, and the method becomes clear. In particular, I sought means to settle the mind quickly, to make it open and unobstructed. The average person's mind is closed and selfish. When the mind is settled, it opens up. With practice it is possible to control emotions and vexations as they come up in daily life. I familiarized myself with these methods to help myself as well as others.

I recognized the three fundamental principles of Buddhism — precepts, samadhi, and wisdom. I started to study the Vinaya, which spells out the precepts, or rules of conduct for monks and nuns. Precepts are guidelines to living within the teaching of the Buddha. Without a firm basis in the precepts, practicing samadhi can lead to outer paths, or to perverse views and behavior. Precepts protect us and keep us on the right path.

I also read a lot of scriptures. When I didn't have a master, I took the scriptures as my master, reasoning that if my views did not accord with the sutras, I would recognize my mistakes. Previously, when I read the sutras, I saw many contradictions. For example, each sutra was presented as the true teaching. But how could this be? These contradictions fell away when I saw that they represented different levels of the teaching of the Dharma. The Buddha taught different things to different people according to their experience and levels of attainment.

When I went to Taiwan, I was recruited into the army. Soon, however, I wished to take on a monk's robe again. There was a master, Tung-Ch'u, whom I sensed to be an extraordinary individual. He did not lecture, nor did he give people instruction in practice. Seeking neither fame nor followers, he was widely known and respected. His speech was unusual and had a startling effect on people. He was heir to both the Lin-chi and Ts'ao-tung traditions of Ch'an. Later, I found out that when we met, he wished to have me as a student but did not express it. As it turned out, I did become his disciple.

My stay with him turned out to be one of the most difficult periods of my life. He constantly harassed me. It reminded me of the treatment that Milarepa received from his guru Marpa. For example, after telling me to move my things into one room, he would later tell me to move to another room. Then he would tell me to move back again. Once, he told me to seal off a door and to open a new one in another wall. I had to haul the bricks by foot from a distant kiln up to the monastery. We normally used a gas stove, but my master often sent me to the mountains to gather a special kind of firewood that he liked to brew his tea over. I would constantly be scolded for cutting the wood too small or too large. I had many experiences of this kind.

In my practice it was much the same. When I asked him how to practice, he would tell me to meditate. But after a few days he would quote a famous master, saying, "You can't make a mirror by polishing a brick, and you can't become a Buddha by sitting." So he ordered me to do prostrations. Then, after several days, he would say "This is nothing but a dog eating shit off the ground. Read the sutras!" After I read for a couple of weeks, he would scold me again, saying that the patriarchs thought the sutras good only for cleaning sores. He would say, "You're smart. Write an essay." When I showed him an essay he would tear it up saying, "These are all stolen ideas." Then he would challenge me to use my own wisdom and say original things.

When I lived with him, he forbade me to keep a blanket, because monks were supposed to meditate at night. When tired, we could nap, but were not to rely on the comfort of a bed or blanket. These arbitrary rules and orders were actually his way of training me. Whatever I did was wrong even if he had just told me to do it. Although it was hard to think of this treatment as compassionate, it really was. If I hadn't been trained with this kind of discipline, I would not have accomplished much. I also realized from my time with him that learning the Buddha Dharma was a very vigorous activity, and that one should be self-reliant in practice.

After two years with Master Tung-Ch'u, I went into solitary retreat in the mountains. When I left I told him that I vowed to practice hard and not fail the Dharma. He answered, "Wrong! What is Buddhism? What is Dharma? The most important thing is not to fail yourself!"

Once Master Tung-Ch'u told me, "The relationship between a master and disciple is like that of father and son, like teacher and student, but it is also a friendship. The master may guide, criticize, and correct, but the disciple must be responsible for his own practice. The master cannot worry over his disciple like a mother. The master just leads the disciple onto the Path; the disciple must walk the Path himself."

Finally Master Tung-Ch'u told me that a practitioner must emphasize both wisdom and merit. Practicing alone, one can cultivate samadhi and wisdom, but he must remember that there are sentient beings needing the nourishment of Buddha Dharma. He said, "Control yourself. When you can control yourself, you can freely harmonize with the multitudes."

The first half year of my retreat, I emphasized repentance prostration to undo my heavy karma. I first prostrated through the Lotus Sutra; later, the Avatamsaka Sutra. After reading a character, I would recite a mantra and then prostrate. The mantras were "Na mo fa-hua hui-shang fo p'u-'sa" ("Homage to the Buddhas and Bodhisattvas of the Lotus Assembly") for Lotus Sutra, and "Na mo hua-yen hai-hui fo p'u-sa" ("Homage to the Buddhas and Bodhisattvas of the ocean of wisdom of the Avatamsaka Sutra.") for the Avatamsaka Sutra. This I did through the whole sutra. After prostrating for five hours I would meditate. On other occasions I practiced reciting Amitabha Buddha's name.

From the moment I started the retreat, my mind was very calm and settled, never restless. I felt very happy, as though I had come home. I ate one meal a day of leaves from wild potatoes, which I had planted myself. I lived in a hut with a yard. There were walls behind, but the front looked out on a cliff. Even though I always remained in the courtyard, I never had a feeling of being closed in.

Eventually I began to prostrate less, spending more time meditating and reading sutras. I also wrote a lot. Six years passed very quickly; I had little sense of time. I hadn't accomplished what I had hoped to, but others persistently urged me to return, so I left the mountains. Returning to Taipei, I still felt inadequate. I thought that to teach Buddha Dharma in this age, I needed a modern education and a degree. So I made plans to study in Japan. The preparation took close to one year. Meanwhile I continued to lecture and write.

At the age of thirty-eight I went to Japan and started work towards a doctorate in Buddhist Literature. This I did in the relatively short time of six years. I attribute this not to any native intelligence, but to the discipline of practice, and to the compassion of Kuan Yin Bodhisattva. During this time, I had financial problems, and many times was ready to return to Taiwan. My advisor, who was also a practitioner, said, "In clothing and food there is no mind for the Path, but with a mind for the Path there will always be food and clothing." After hearing this, I made daily prostrations to Kuan Yin. Oddly enough, after a short while, I started to receive annual donations from someone in Switzerland, which were sufficient to cover my tuition and the costs to publish my dissertation. To this day I don't know who the donor was.

During this period, I visited various masters of Zen and esoteric Buddhism. I received the greatest influence from Bantetsugu Roshi, a disciple of Harada Roshi. I attended several winter-long retreats at his temple in Tohoku. Being in northern Japan, the temple had a very harsh environment. Moreover, the master seemed inclined to give me an especially hard time and constantly had his assistants beat me. Of the people there I had by far the most education, and he would say, "You scholars have a lot of selfish attachments and vexations. Your obstructions are heavy."

When I was leaving him he said, "Go to America and teach there." I replied, "But master, I don't know English." He said, "Zen doesn't rely on words. Why worry about words?"

Editor's note: Master Sheng-yen has received Dharma transmission in the two major braches of Ch'an Buddhism, the Lin-Chi (Japanese Rinzai), and the Ts'ao-Tung (Japanese Soto). In genealogical terms, Master Sheng-yen is a seventy-second generation descendant of Bodhidharma (?-ca.530), the First Patriarch of Ch'an, and the sixty-seventh generation descendant of Hui-Neng (638-713), the Sixth Patriarch of Ch'an. Within the Lin-Chi lineage, Master Sheng-yen is a sixty-second generation descendant of Master Lin-Chi(?-866), and a third-generation descendant of Master Hsu-Yun (1840-1959). In this line, he is the direct descendant of master Ling-Yuan (1902-1988).

In the Ts'ao-Tung lineage, Master Sheng-yen is the fiftieth-generation descendant of co-founder Master Tung-Shan (807-869), and the direct descendant of Master Tung-Ch'u (1908-1977).

"Generation" refers to the transmission of the Dharma within a lineage from a master to a disciple. This transmission thereby ensures the continuity not only of the Dharma itself, but also the teaching and the practice of the lineage. Furthermore, it confers upon the recipient a recognition by the master that the disciple is now qualified to transmit the Dharma, i.e., has become a master.

The Ch'an Seven-day Retreat

The seven-day retreat, or "Ch'an seven," is a practice in which disciples gather for a period of intense meditation under the guidance of a Ch'an master. The attitude of disciples during this period is one of total dedication to the task at hand — to shed, at least for a period of time, all the vexations of mind and body, and to bring the mind to a state of supreme clarity.

Since Sakyamuni Buddha, there has been a tradition of setting aside a definite period for deep practice. The aim is to achieve realization within that period. We learn from the Buddhist sutras that there were various periods, ranging from seven days to fourteen, twenty-one, or forty-nine days, always a multiple of seven days. In some cases this period lasted as long as three months. Of course it was only when Buddhism entered China that the term "Ch'an retreat" developed. (The Chinese word *ch'an* is derived from the Sanskrit *dhyana*, and the Japanese *zen* in turn, from *ch'an*.) In fact, what we call a Ch'an retreat literally means "Ch'an seven." In the Pure

Land sect the practice of reciting the Buddha's name for seven days is called "Buddha seven." Reciting Kuan Yin's name for seven days is "Kuan Yin seven." Some people practice repentance-prostration for seven days, and that would be "repentance seven." These are periods when one practices with more dedication and energy than usual, with the goal of achieving significant results.

Why seven days or a multiple of seven days? Our mental states are influenced by our physical states, which in turn are influenced by the cosmos. Nature itself seems to take seven days as a definite period. This concept of seven days is very ancient. It may come from the observation of celestial bodies. In the Bible, God created the world in seven days. In India the seven days of the week were related to the seven planets. In ancient China this period was called "one come-and-go."

Our body is a small universe, a microcosm, and it tends to reflect the great universe, the macrocosm. Our body and mind seem to demonstrate a cycle of seven days. Thus we take seven days as the optimum period of practice. Therefore, we can use the seven day cycle to help us to get onto a smooth and diligent path of practice. In Japan it is called *sesshin*, meaning "uniting, or transmitting, the mind." This can be interpreted on one hand, as the roshi, or teacher, taking away the student's vexed mind and enabling him to achieve enlightenment. On the other hand, the student takes the mind from the roshi.

What is it that is transmitted from master to disciple, generation after generation? It is Buddha-mind. When a person has eliminated his vexations, that is called "getting the Buddha-mind." We also use the phrase "seeing one's self-nature," or "seeing one's original face." The person who has entered the Path has done so because he wants to break the endless cycle of suffering. At the moment of enlightenment, he is clear of vexation and has received the Buddha-mind. So "transmission" means both that the student has had a Buddha-mind experience and that the experience was recognized by a master. Although it is said that the Buddha-mind has been "transmitted" from Sakyamuni to master to disciple, it is really the disciple who, through faith and practice, has developed on his own that Buddha-mind. To confirm the transmission, there must be an experienced master who can recognize the student's achievement. There are not many formal records of Ch'an retreats, but a few famous cases have come down from the Sung Dynasty. In one of these, Master Ta-Hui held a retreat in which thirteen out of fifty-three became enlightened. Another master, Yuan-Wu, transmitted to eighteen disciples in one night. This gives you some idea of the power of the Ch'an retreat in the hands of a great master.

Because the traditional retreat had many participants, there was little opportunity to speak with the master. In fact, the master would usually come into the hall only to say a few words. Most disciples would not dare ask for a private interview unless he had an experience he wanted to have affirmed. In modern times, the Ch'an master has been more accessible. In Japan the *dokusan*, or interview, is actually required by many masters. In any event, it is in the interview that recognition usually takes place. More often than not, the student is not confirmed and sometimes even receives a stinging rebuke or a beating. This is done not to punish, but to provoke the student to greater effort or to break through obstructions. The technique is used by the master according to his perception of the student's state of mind. To a Ch'an master, even the way a student prostrates can show a presence or lack of genuine achievement.

In Sakyamuni's time there were disciples who got enlightened, but didn't know it, and others who thought they did, but in fact didn't. It was necessary for Sakyamuni himself, or one of his major disciples, to recognize and confirm the disciples. Therefore, to attain the Buddha-mind and to be confirmed are strong reasons for participating in retreats.

To one who has not received the Buddha-mind, it seems very mysterious. Even people who have had a glimpse cannot always recognize it. This recognition cannot be explained, but can only be done by one who has already experienced it at a deep level. A good master has had many deep experiences and frequently can ascertain someone's level of attainment just by looking at him. Very often affirmation comes through master and disciple asking each other questions, or the disciple describing his experiences to the master. One who has seen self-nature for the first time could not recognize another's experience, nor is he ready to accept disciples.

The chance of a practitioner getting the Buddha-mind depends on his developing a "great ball of doubt," which drives him to diligent and energetic practice. During retreat the master tries to bring each student to this state of great doubt, for only then is it possible to create an opening through which the Buddha-mind can enter. The Ch'an master will use different methods to do this, according to the student's state of mind, personality, and accomplishment. So how I deal with a student depends on my sense of the student's mental state. I call this a spontaneous perception-response. I don't reflect on how I should deal with each student. I don't form an idea that one student needs this, another needs that. If it is time to scold or strike, I scold or strike. If it is time to console or encourage, I console or encourage. I am just a mirror. The student's perception of me is a perception of him or herself.

At the start of retreat, the students' minds are usually scattered. The concerns of daily life are still with them. They may have fears and anticipations about being on retreat. A cold, pains, bodily complaints — all add to the more or less uneven states of mind. At this point it is necessary to give them methods that will help them settle down and become concentrated. I often have them start with simple methods, such as counting or following the breath. The reason is most modern lay people lack a firm foundation in practice. Only when their mind has settled will I give them a kung-an to help generate the doubt sensation. Only then is there a chance for enlightenment. Even without enlightenment, when doubt has formed, the student has at least gotten on the proper path of practice.

At the beginning, kung-an can be used as a method to help the students settle their minds. It is more like reciting a mantra, simply repeating the phrase, over and over. This can help to gather a scattered mind, but it takes a long time before a student can truly work with the kung-an. This is when the kung-an is not a mechanically repeated phrase, but becomes a deeply felt question whose answer has life-and-death urgency, but which cannot be found by reasoning. When this happens, when there is no thought other than the kung-an, the doubt sensation can be generated. Only then can the mind open up for an experience. This stage may be reached naturally after a period of time, or it may come about from suggestions made by the master.

In the Ts'ao-tung sect, neither breathing methods nor kung-an are used in the beginning. Instead, the method called "silent illumination," the "method of no method," is used. Because the method dispenses with technique, it requires tremendous concentration and energy to penetrate into the fundamental emptiness of the mind. In this method even the mind itself is seen as formless. In Japan, this is practiced by the Soto sect and is known as *shikantaza.*

By judging the student's mental state, and knowing when to assign or suggest a method, the master can help the student generate the energy for practice. With the right conditions, with dedication and hard work under a watchful master, it is possible in seven days to make considerable progress, even to experience one's self-nature. From the point of view of a struggling student, to say that getting some experience is very difficult is accurate, there are people who have practiced for decades before getting genuine results. So in comparison, getting an experience in seven days can be considered easy; it is just seven days compared to decades. Of course, you should not think that it is too easy.

Those fortunate enough to have some genuine experience find that the results do not necessarily stay with them. If it is not reinforced with practice. over a period of time there is a fading away of the experience. This is quite common. Even monks and nuns can lose the energy of a deep experience, but it is much more difficult for lay people to retain it. In Ch'an there is a verse:

> *To hear the Buddha Dharma is not very difficult.*
> *More difficult is it to practice.*
> *To practice is not very difficult.*
> *More difficult is it to realize the Path.*

To realize the Path is not very difficult.
More difficult is it to not fall from the Path.

There is also a saying: "When you have gotten the Buddha-mind, go to the woods, live by a stream, and meditate. Thus will you nourish your saintly embryo." When will this baby be born? You don't know. But, like an expectant mother, you must nourish the saintly embryo.

To have experienced the Buddha-mind and lost it is a great pity. Even so, to see self-nature is to be forever changed. What is the taste of a mango? If you have never tasted a mango, you can't imagine it. But having tasted it, you still have a memory of it, however faint. Likewise, someone who has experienced Buddha-mind has been changed forever. If he falls from the Path, he is very aware of it, and in his mind there is always the intention to regain the practice. By comparison, one who has never glimpsed Buddha-mind is confused.

PART
TWO

Ch'an Retreat Lectures

Four Conditions for Practicing Ch'an

To investigate the ultimate Ch'an, you should fulfill four conditions. If these conditions are met, it is possible to realize the highest aims of Ch'an. Short of these, your path is uncertain, and progress is difficult. But these conditions must come spontaneously out of your practice. A master can't force them on you or even give them to you. Arising from within, they can be fulfilled more quickly. A master can only lead a disciple onto the Path. The disciple must follow the Path himself. I can only tell you what these requirements are and why they are necessary. The rest is up to you.

When you enter the Path, if you are full of zeal, these conditions arise very naturally. But don't expect them all at once. You must first begin to practice. As you make progress, they will gradually, or in some cases, quickly, be fulfilled. Much depends on your causes and conditions. Therefore, at the beginning of a retreat, I do not mention these requirements. I will only talk about them when I see that people are physically and mentally ready to investigate Ch'an.

What are these four conditions? The first is Great Faith; the second is Great Vow; the third is Great Angry Determination; and the fourth is Great Doubt. Great Faith always arises first, followed by Great Vow, and then Great Angry Determination. When there is Great Angry Determination, it is then possible to generate Great Doubt. This is their natural sequence. But Great Doubt is not an ordinary doubt of disbelief. Only when there is Great Faith is it possible to have Great Doubt. Were you to have ordinary doubt at such a time, it could only be a sort of suspicion or non-belief, the opposite of faith. That kind of doubt is not a condition of practice; it is an obstacle.

Again, without Great Faith, you cannot make the Great Vow. Without Great Vow, how can you practice with your whole being? And if you cannot do that, Great Angry Determination cannot possibly arise. Therefore these four conditions must come into being in the proper sequence.

Faith is the foundation for anything we set out to do. Without faith we can't accomplish anything significant. The Great Faith of Ch'an has three aspects: faith in yourself, faith in the method discovered and transmitted by Sakyamuni Buddha and faith in your Shih-fu, who is your direct connection to the Buddha Dharma. What is faith in oneself? It means believing that you can practice effectively, believing that persistence will lead to enlightenment. It means believing that you can, like Sakyamuni, eventually become a Buddha. If you lack this faith, if you think that enlightenment can only happen to others, your practice will falter. So faith in yourself is very basic.

How does this faith arise? At first it is hard to believe that you can be enlightened. However, if you are willing to try it, when you start to practice, you find your mind getting calm and settled. You may later get some other benefits, or even experience things not possible in ordinary life. You begin to believe: "Yes, I too can practice, I too can become enlightened." Another way of generating faith is to acquire a good understanding of Buddha Dharma, of the principles of Ch'an, and to believe that these principles are true. You come to accept the idea that one can practice and get enlightened. You have never experienced it yourself, but you have an unconditional belief in it.

Great faith, like the other conditions, is deeply related to what I describe as going from a "small" sense of self to a "large" sense of self and finally to a state of "no-self." Great Faith starts with faith in oneself — you first have to affirm the very narrow sense of self. After all, who is it that must have faith? It is "I" who must have faith. So you must start with grasping the narrow sense of self. You must know this self in a very clear and solid manner and be confident that you can practice. This grasping of one's "small self" is the basis of the power of faith.

The second aspect of faith is faith in the method. I often encourage my students with a

Chinese saying: "Once you're on a pirate ship, the best thing to do is become a pirate." You have no choice, because if you are trapped on a pirate ship, and you don't join them, you will probably be killed on the spot. If you join them, you may survive. So once you have accepted the method, you should believe in it, and practice in a single-minded, concentrated manner. You should know that this method was taught by Sakyamuni Buddha. Since he was a Buddha, the original patriarch of Buddhism, and a great human being, he would not teach us a false method. Though you may not have gotten any benefit yet, you still should have faith in it.

In the beginning this is not easy. After using the method their master has given them, some people feel they want a different, hopefully better, method. Actually, every method is the best method. There is no method which is especially good for a particular person, and there is no method that is especially useless to someone. The basic methods are suitable for most people. It is only after you have been practicing for a while that you should think about changing your method. The important thing is to have patience. As long as you put time and genuine effort into it, any of the methods of Ch'an will yield powerful results. If you don't persist, how will you know if the method is effective? If your practice has not matured, how can you know if the method is suitable? In practice the rule is to stick with the method your Shih-fu gives you. Some people are avid for techniques. They may learn a few methods from a master, pick some up from books or friends, and they use them one after the other. Each new technique seems to go very well, but after a while the mind gets scattered, so they find another one. These people are like the farmer in a Chinese fable who is worried that his rice crop is not growing fast enough, so he went around pulling at the shoots to encourage them to grow. Of course he only succeeded in uprooting them, and the next day when he checked again, the plants were dead. Don't be an anxious farmer; be patient. If you are, you will definitely get results. After getting even a little bit of benefit, you will feel very relaxed and blissful in mind and body, and your faith will grow, motivating you to practice very hard.

The third aspect of faith is faith in Shih-fu. It is very difficult to have complete faith in a master you have met for the first time on retreat. If the master is very famous, some people may feel that since everybody has faith in him, they should also. But the faith of most people can only be partial. They think that the master can help them, but just how much, they are not sure. They are willing to give him a chance. On the other hand, what this master says and does may be quite different from what they imagined a master should say and do. So doubts naturally arise.

For this reason, I never ask people to have complete faith in me at the start of retreat. Only after the practitioners have experienced some results do they begin to feel that I can help them. At that point, they are willing to follow my instructions. This faith in Shih-fu is extremely important. If you doubt the master, wondering whether he is capable or has an ulterior motive, it is impossible to gain genuine results. You should not even bother to practice with him. To have faith in Shih-fu is to have faith in his instructions. It is not that Shih-fu wants you to think of him as a deity, rather you should believe that Shih-fu has the ability and experience to help your practice.

If you are lost at sea or in the desert, you can become as helpless as a baby. So having faith in your Shih-fu is like having a compass to guide you when you are lost. At that time you don't know anything, and if you cling to your own viewpoint and judgment, you will remain lost.

We often say that practice can incite demonic states. These demons do not come from without; they come from within — from thoughts that are contradictory, impure, incorrect, leading you to a worse and worse state. Under these circumstances, after practice has borne some fruit, you have an even greater need for complete faith in Shih-fu. Whatever he tells you to do, you should do. If he tells you to take a rest, you cannot say, "I am very energetic now. I want to continue." If he tells you to practice harder, you cannot say, "I'm feeling lousy now. I want to rest." It is not that Shih-fu is a dictator, but under these circumstances, his experience tells him what is happening, and he is the only one capable of helping you.

In China when you entered the Ch'an hall, it was demanded that you give up your body to the monastery and your life to the "dragons and devas" — the Dharma protectors. But in fact, both the monastery and the Dharma protectors are personified by the master. If you disregard Shih-fu, it is like a pilot disregarding the directions of the control tower. If he disobeys, disasters will happen. So Shih-fu is like a compass or control tower. Time and again, he corrects and adjusts your practice, leading you forward. You should understand that this faith in Shih-fu is really faith in the Buddha Dharma which Shih-fu represents. You must believe in him one hundred percent. Forget your past and future. Don't cling to any viewpoints. Let Shih-fu guide you in all aspects of the practice.

The Great Vow is setting up and defining the goal. Without a goal, we may go in circles or backwards. But if we have a view of the proper goal, whether we travel fast or slow, eventually we reach our destination. This is the first aspect of the Great Vow. The second aspect is that the Great Vow helps us overcome selfishness. We make vows not for our own sake but for the sake of all sentient beings.

Sakyamuni became the Buddha because he saw that all life is full of suffering — birth, aging, sickness, death. He also saw that in the animal realm the weaker animals are preyed upon by the stronger animals. He realized that *samsara*, the cycle of birth and death, is characterized by suffering. To him the question of helping sentient beings to liberate themselves from this suffering became very crucial. He decided to give up his royal position and dedicate himself to finding a way to help all sentient beings. Therefore he made a vow to leave home and become an ascetic. After practicing many methods for many years, he became supremely enlightened, and attained Buddhahood. If he was selfishly motivated, after his liberation, Sakyamuni Buddha would not have stayed behind to teach others. But within a few days he started teaching and these teachings have been handed down until today. His vow helped him to attain Buddhahood. This Great Vow is very different from selfishness. It is not just thinking, "I want to be enlightened." That attitude is good for developing faith in one's self. But by the time one develops the Great Vow one should gradually drop this self-centeredness.

At this point the expanded, "large" sense of self appears. Great Vow is needed to transcend the "small" self. If we are not willing to leave behind this self, it is impossible to get enlightened. That can only come after you have let go of the self, and perceived *"wu"* (emptiness) or "no-self." It is for this reason that all Buddhas made Great Vows when they began their practice. The most common vows we make are the Four Great Vows:

I vow to help all sentient beings.
I vow to cut off all vexations.
I vow to master all Dharma methods.
I vow to reach Buddhahood.

The first vow is the most important. If you think only of helping sentient beings, naturally your own vexations will be lessened. If you have only helping sentient beings in mind, naturally you will learn all the Dharma methods. Finally, if you persist in helping sentient beings until there is no self, at that time sentient beings also disappear. Then you will have attained Buddhahood, for at that point there is no discrimination, no sentient beings, and no self. These vows are made every day by all Buddhas and Bodhisattvas and anyone who wishes to practice seriously. Of course we cannot accomplish these vows on retreat, but we can derive great energy from them. The power of the vows pulls us ahead, because they are always kept in front of us.

Other than these Great Vows, another vow that I emphasize is one that should be made before each sitting. Before his enlightenment, when Sakyamuni sat down on his pile of dry grass, he made a vow. He said, "I will not rise until I reach the supreme awakening, though my body becomes as dust." In later ages, his seat was considered the "diamond seat," in reference to the unmoving nature of his mind. Each time we sit, though we may not accomplish the diamond seat, it should at least be a stone seat. It should not be a seat of whipped cream. Before each sitting, we should vow to sit until we get to a certain state. Will such vows always be accomplished? Not often. Your legs really hurt, your mind is scattered, you can't meditate anymore. What can you do? You give up. Then you tell yourself, this time I failed in my vow. But next time, I will make the same vow, and do better. With each sitting, making such a vow, your sittings improve, your faith and energy grow.

Great Angry Determination is not a kind of hate, but rather, has to do with the will. It is also different from the Great Vow. Great Angry Determination is the persistence to practice hard, to go forward continuously. Basically, everybody has great inertia. When they run into difficulties, they can be disillusioned and disappointed. When tired they want to sleep. Practice is like rowing a boat upstream. If you don't row continuously, you will drift backward. When you cook rice, you cook it until it is ready, in one cooking. If you cook it for a while, turn off the fire, then later, turn on the fire again, and so on; you definitely won't get good rice. Just like in practice. You do it consistently, not interruptedly.

There are people who work so hard that they forget to sleep or eat. And not just practitioners. For example, a scientist trying to solve a problem will forget all about daily life and work single-mindedly on a project. Most people, long before forgetting their environment, and forgetting sleep and food, are more likely to slack off, take a break, and relax their efforts. This is why we need Great Angry Determination — to overcome inertia and laxity.

The Great Vow pulls us forward while Great Angry Determination pushes us from behind. But how do we generate Great Angry Determination? A lot of people simply let their anger out, show their temper, or hate themselves, thinking that this is Great Angry Determination. But it is not, especially if Great Faith and Great Vow are lacking. Great Angry Determination can arise from thinking: "I haven't done justice to Sakyamuni Buddha. He suffered tremendously to discover the Path for helping all sentient beings, and transmitted it to us. Now that I am on this same Path how can I not strive as hard as I can?" Thinking this way, if we still do not practice hard, we should prostrate in remorse to Sakyamuni Buddha.

The second thing I should emphasize is how rare it is to be born a human being who hears the Buddha Dharma. Imagine! Out of all the people in the world, I am one who has learned of the Path and want to follow it. I should realize how rare it is to have such good karma, and throw my whole self into the practice. I should make the best use of my time and good fortune.

The third thing I should realize is how lucky I am to have a good environment to practice in and to have met someone who is qualified to guide me. If I don't work now, when will I do it? If I am a lay person, I should realize that while monks and nuns can practice their whole life, I have fewer opportunities to practice. This is all the more reason to strive very hard.

The fourth thought is to realize the shortness of life. I don't know when I'm going to die. Were I to die now, without accomplishing my practice, it would be very unfortunate. If I have only one spurt of energy left, I should put that energy into practice. Whether I can get enlightened or not is another question. At least I haven't failed myself; I've done justice to myself. And in the next life, I can probably continue practicing. If I were to die in idleness, in my next birth my karma may not be so good as to allow me to continue practicing. Recognizing the shortness of life and seeing how I must do justice to myself, I should put my whole being into practice. Great Angry Determination is actually this attitude of great earnestness and great diligence.

Most people cannot generate this Angry Determination, nor can they pretend to have it. If they try to generate it, their minds will be very confused and scattered, and they will have a lot of vexations. You should know that after practicing for sometime, when one has Great Faith and Great Vow, when one's mind is settled, when one's health is good, it is possible to slip into idleness and looseness. In such a situation, one should still try to generate Angry Determination. Just thinking will not make it happen, but you will at least be alert to your condition, and that can help you move forward again. But unless the two previous conditions are already fulfilled, trying to arouse Angry Determination can only produce scatteredness, vexation, and anger. This may result in disappointment and disillusion, but not Angry Determination.

We come now to Great Doubt. Great Doubt is possible, or is forceful, only when the mind is very stable and unified. At this point, you will probably be using a hua-t'ou or kung-an. In most cases these practices come from tradition, recorded and handed down by patriarchs and masters, but not always. It is possible for you as a practitioner to spontaneously generate a question, a great doubt, in your mind. And in such a situation you can simply pursue the hua-t'ou which arises spontaneously. So what is Great Doubt? It is a question, whose answer is of the utmost importance to the practitioner. His attitude is one of great anxiousness to find the answer. And yet he cannot use reasoning or logic, or rely on his knowledge or experience. He can only pursue the question, and continue questioning without interruption.

Originally Ch'an masters did not use recorded hua-t'ous. These simply occurred spontaneously. Later, these happenings were recorded as "kung-ans," and handed down to later generations to "investigate." In the ancient days the masters guided the disciples to the point where hua-t'ous occurred spontaneously. Later generations used these recorded kung-ans when they could not generate the questions by themselves. But kung-ans or hua-t'ous can produce Great Doubt only if one's mind is already in a unified state, only when one has already a strong foundation of practice. Otherwise, it can become just a mechanical repetition, producing no useful effect whatsoever. And very likely the practitioner will be using reasoning, knowledge, and experience to find an answer. This is neither the Great Doubt, nor is it investigating Ch'an.

So it is possible to practice kung-ans before your mind is unified and concentrated, but it will not produce the Great Doubt. I will not give you a kung-an in the very beginning. I will wait until you have a certain foundation before giving you a kung-an, or helping you generate your own.

Therefore one must wait until the student's mind is settled, and then it is possible to explode this settled, unified mind. I describe the process as starting with scattered mind, then using a method to unify the scattered mind into samadhi, and finally applying the method of Ch'an to dissolve the unified state. A scattered mind lacks the focus and energy necessary for this great event. It must first be collected and concentrated. Then, at that stage, you need the power of Great Doubt to cause a great explosion, and enter the enlightened state.

The unified mind is like a balloon. As you inflate it steadily with pressure, it will yield and expand. If you continue without letting up, at a certain point it will expand no more, and explode. So when the mind is in a unified state, it is ready to generate the Great Doubt. This doubt can be generated by the hua-t'ou — the great question that must be answered: "What is *Wu?*" "Who am I?" "What is my original face?" "What is the meaning of this kung-an?" But you must continue without stopping, without letting in stray thoughts. When you're blowing up a balloon, you can't blow a few breaths, then let the air out, then start up again. This way you'd never get it to stretch to the maximum point. When people are in samadhi they may feel that there is no mind, no thoughts. But even in that state there is a mind left. It's just that you are not aware of it. One is not aware of this sense of "large self." But you must lose even this to be genuinely enlightened. At that stage there is no problem of "small" or "large" sense of self, no more attachment or vexations, no more greed, hate, ignorance, pride, doubt. In the state of one-mind, there is still a sense of self. But after the explosion, even this sense of expanded self is gone, though everything still exists.

So if there is a sense of "I love sentient beings, I want to help sentient beings," this is not ultimate enlightenment. Genuine enlightenment means being liberated from concepts of self, as well as of sentient beings.

As in Great Angry Determination, before one is sufficiently calm and stable, one should not try to generate this Great Doubt. Great Doubt would not arise, and it would most likely result in a scattered mind. Even worse, it would create a lot of anxiety. And when you're overanxious you can't even reach samadhi, much less get enlightened. A person may not have a settled mind and yet anxiously seek an answer. To be hoping for an answer is all right, but to be anxious can be bad. To be overanxious is a great obstruction to practice. So without a reliable Shih-fu, a person should not try to generate Great Angry Determination or Great Doubt. One will lead to anger without determination, and the other to anxiety, both bad for practice.

On the other hand, if you are pursuing Great Doubt in a mild or lukewarm manner, this could lead to scattered mind, or at best you may enter samadhi. So while anxiousness is bad, Great Doubt cannot be raised in a casual way. The hua-t'ou must be followed with energy, persistence, without let-up, in every act, through every moment of practice. Eventually the Ch'an power accumulates, and the door of Ch'an can be entered.

It is hoped that all who go on retreat can fulfill the four conditions. In reality, there will be a few who can begin to fulfill them. For most, this is not possible. Often people can fulfill Great Faith, which can then give rise to Great Vow, but the last two require persistence and practice. Practice is not like giving an injection to a patient to get quick results. It takes time and patience, and the power and energy must come from within. It must be a part of your life.

If you're just curious to try Ch'an for a while, that can bring you some benefit, but such a casual approach will never fulfill the four conditions for investigating Ch'an; it can never lead you to the ultimate Ch'an.

Selflessness

To find your real self, you must lose yourself. I tell my students that they must put aside thoughts about their own birth and death if they are to get anywhere. Meditators who are full of thoughts about themselves, thoughts of improving their health, or of gaining limitless freedom, will attain neither wisdom nor freedom.

The self derives from the three poisons – desire, aggression and delusion. Practicing Ch'an, you can gradually eliminate these three poisons. As the poisons are eliminated, you acquire wisdom and dissolve the false concept of self, so that your true self-nature is revealed. At that point, you discover that self-nature is selflessness. Having reached this stage, you know what is meant by living Buddhism and true self-nature.

While the self ultimately needs to be dissolved, in the meantime, we need this self to help us reach selflessness. To think of being selfless from the very beginning, without having gone through the path of practice, is called "wild fox Ch'an." Just as a baby must crawl before it can walk, you must begin with your ordinary self before finding self-nature. From there you proceed by stages of practice to wisdom. Therefore you should understand why we must start the practice with our ordinary, selfish self. It is not to be despised; it is your vehicle to selflessness.

Non-Opposition

Buddhism condemns fighting and advocates non-opposition to one's enemies. This principle also applies to meditation. When you meditate, vexations and scattered thoughts may arise. You may be hindered by bad habits, or disturbed by noises. If these problems annoy you, no matter where you are, you will be unable to settle your mind and practice Ch'an. You have merely added another layer of scattered thoughts to your original set. The result is wasted effort. If you do this habitually, the more you meditate the more disturbed and ill-tempered you will become. This is why many so-called "old cultivators" have very irritable dispositions and become angry at the slightest provocation. This is due to their wrong approach of opposing, fighting against their vexations and scattered thoughts, thus increasing their problems and creating much internal tension.

A true Ch'an practitioner handles distractions or unfavorable conditions with non-opposition, without resisting. What is meant by non-opposition? For example, if someone treats you maliciously, you would not wrangle with him. Rather, you would do everything to peacefully avoid a confrontation. In this way the dissolving of tensions is most likely to be achieved. It's the same when practicing Ch'an. Don't be disturbed by scattered thoughts. If you don't desire the pleasant, or repulse the unpleasant, your mind will naturally become collected. Ch'an practitioners should also maintain this attitude during their daily life. To become annoyed when faced with difficulties merely adds difficulty to difficulty. By maintaining a mind of peace and non-opposition, all tensions will naturally be dissolved.

Stages of Emptiness

Emptiness and existence are coextensive; there is no barrier between the two. Yet practitioners have difficulty finding their way from existence to emptiness. They can't go from phenomena back to the basis of their being: emptiness. In meditation, we go from phenomena to emptiness by progressively voiding our mental states.

When you came to this retreat, I told you to bundle up all your everyday thoughts and habits — everything connected to your life — and leave them outside. This is the first kind of voiding — leaving behind your preoccupations. On the first day I said that we have a very noisy environment for practice — cars, radios, kids, and so on — and I asked if the noises outside would bother you. Most people said "No." Later, one student said that the outside sounds didn't bother her, only my words did. She couldn't stop thinking about them. If I told everyone to relax, she would just sit there saying to herself: "Relax, relax, relax." If I told everyone to be like a corpse, she would think, "I am dead, I am dead." She said, "I can put down everything except Shih-fu's words." I told you to bow to your cushion before you sit and vow to sit well. But after you sit, forget it.

There was another student who kept wishing to meditate well. But as long as he kept wishing, he was not meditating, and certainly not meditating well. So the second level is to void out thoughts that come up in the course of the retreat.

To progress to a further stage of voiding, you must next forget the meditation method itself. It's like putting on a pair of glasses. The normal thing is just to forget you are wearing them and just see through them. If you're always conscious of the glasses, that will be troublesome to you. Another example would be an athlete who spends years training. But when he plays in actual competition, he has to forget his techniques and just play. To make real progress in meditation, at some point you have to forget the method and just meditate. Nearly everyone here has the problem of not being able to forget the method. This can be a real burden.

When you are just using the method and not thinking about it, you have voided one big mental factor. Now go one step further and forget yourself too. It's like a man so engrossed in watching a pretty girl walk down the street, that he forgets himself and steps right into a puddle. When you forget yourself, you have no standpoint, no sense of body. If you were to forget the method but not yourself, your body would feel very comfortable. But when you forget yourself, feelings of comfort or discomfort don't matter, yet everything around you continues to exist with clarity.

Finally you must forget even the environment. Though your ears are not stopped, you hear nothing; though your eyes are open, you see nothing. You have no sense of time. Having voided your outside problems, your present thoughts, your method, your self, your surroundings, you have entered samadhi.

To reach this point is a major obstacle for most people. If you can at least forget the method, you will lose awareness of time and sit very well. If you can forget yourself, you may experience a personality change. If you can then forget the environment and enter samadhi, you will definitely undergo a big change. You will have moved a long way from phenomena to emptiness. At that time I will give you a method to go beyond that, to the stage of "no-self."

To sum up the five levels: First, empty your mind of thoughts of your daily life. Second, put down thoughts coming up during the retreat. Third, void the method itself. Fourth, forget yourself. Fifth, forget the environment. Ask yourself what level you have been able to reach so far.

When I meditate, I go through the same five steps. One by one, I forget the previous level until I reach the fifth level. In the past I would go through this process very slowly. Now I pass very quickly and smoothly through each level. With practice you will be able to do the same. It is written in the sutras that Sakyamuni Buddha would enter into what is called the "levels of *dhyana*" when he meditated. He would enter the first level of *dhyana* before going to the second, the third, and so on. What I am talking about, however, are the levels that reach from the ordinary state of mind to samadhi. This would be equivalent only to the first level of the Buddha's *dhyana*. Of course you're not meditating on the level of the Buddha, but the process is the same.

So with these instructions, you can be very clear about how to practice. When you are working hard, you can see your own practice very clearly. As you move from one level to another you know precisely what the next level is. Like the rungs of a ladder the steps are well marked out. With continued practice you'll eventually ascend very quickly.

The Four Great Barriers

At some point, after diligent practice, you begin to experience things beyond the simple tranquillity that came easily in the early stages. You should know that the path that lies ahead is the same path traveled by the Buddhas and Bodhisattvas, and therefore presents unlimited potential for liberation. Though you may feel at any stage that your achievement is genuine, each attainment is also a barrier, and can be an obstruction to further progress. But each barrier is also an opportunity to progress to the next stage.

For the meditator who is on the path of liberation, there are four great barriers to pass. When I speak of barriers I do not refer to something absolute. Everyone's experience will be unique. At any given time, people are at different stages according to their karma, potential, and effort. I will describe these barriers so you will recognize them, and you will be aware that there can be problems, even at high levels of attainment.

The first barrier is the experience of limitless light and sound. The second is the state of extreme peace and purity. The third is attaining emptiness, enlightenment. The fourth and ultimate barrier is shattering emptiness itself.

The first barrier arises from samadhi, or deep concentration, and comes as an experience of boundless bright light and sounds of music, beyond description, endlessly floating. You feel very clear and very relaxed. You are not beyond time and space, for light exists in space, and music plays in time. But this light and sound seem limitless, and you feel liberated. As long as you are meditating there is no problem. But when you return to the everyday world, you also return to its influence and distractions. You return to attachments. You find that you cannot maintain that state for long.

As your practice strengthens and your samadhi deepens, you may enter the second barrier, a sense of extreme purity and peace. You feel as if you are beyond time and space, as if they didn't exist. In that state a whole day or night could pass in a flash. Many people who enter this state think that they have become enlightened. With even stronger practice, as you work through the second barrier, coming out of samadhi, your mind is pure and peaceful. Vexations don't arise easily. But rarely can this condition be maintained for more than two weeks. After awhile it will begin to fade. This is not to say that every time you sit you can say, "Now I will go into samadhi," and just do it.

Both of these stages can easily be mistaken for

genuine enlightenment, but in fact they are not because there is still attachment. In the first stage there is attachment to the limitless light and sound. At the second stage there is attachment to the feeling of purity and peace. Since you have attachment, it is very difficult to recapture the experience at will. The only thing you can do is forget about it, and start from the very beginning.

On a previous retreat, I described the stages of emptiness in meditation, and how one goes step by step into a deeper state of meditation. The same applies here. It would be impossible to go from the mind of attachment directly to a deep meditative state. You have to start from a shallow meditation and then go progressively deeper and deeper. As you go into these deeper levels, your mind gradually becomes purer, until you reach the point where you are no longer attached. In other words, with proper application of method and technique, even with deep attachment, you can enter these realms of delight. If you don't have a good master to guide you at that point, there are two problems. First, you try to regain the state you once achieved. This is an obstruction to further practice. Second, if you don't have the guidance of a good master, you may assume you've reached the highest stage.

You want to believe that you have reached the ultimate, but in daily life vexations and attachments resurface, and you will experience doubt. "Did I really get enlightened?" After tossing this question around, you may conclude, "Yes, I probably did reach the highest state. Maybe even the great masters didn't go beyond this." Because you have doubt, you try to convince yourself you are at the level of the masters. If you do this, you have given rise to a kind of pride that is hard to uproot.

If you get past the first two barriers, and find yourself approaching the third, you may be on the threshold of genuine enlightenment. But, unlike the first two stages, there are no words for enlightenment. Enlightened people see the world just as it is. Indeed what they see is completely different from what the ordinary person perceives. When they see a leaf they may see the cosmos contained in it. This is not psychic power, nor is it normal knowledge. If you ask them to talk about it, they can say nothing. They would feel neither delight nor aversion. It's just a state of great awakening.

Usually when people reach this stage, they feel they have attained the ultimate, that they have been liberated, like the Buddha, from the cycle of birth and death. It is very good to reach this stage. But if you stop here, there will still be a thought in your mind. That thought is the idea of enlightenment itself, the feeling that you have had the great awakening. You are dwelling in emptiness, and you miss the point.

To get beyond this barrier, we have to go to the fourth and ultimate barrier shattering emptiness itself. In the state of emptiness, one feels that everything exists without obstruction. That is the meaning of emptiness. The meaning of shattering emptiness is dissolving even the enlightened state. You give up the feeling that you've had the great awakening. You will feel ordinary again. Only then will you sleep the dreamless sleep, only then will you be truly liberated.

According to the course of progress of Hinayana Buddhism, you have tasted the fruit of Arhatship. But you still must continue practicing because you still may fall back. You may think, "How can we do all this? It sounds so remote." On the other hand, if I were to tell you that passing the first barrier amounts to great liberation, I would be deceiving you. If you have any doubts, practice hard, and let your doubts grow to the size of a mountain. Remember, small doubt leads to small awakening, great doubt leads to great awakening.

Kung-an Practice

When your practice reaches a certain level, and I perceive that your mind has settled to a degree where you are ready for hard work, I may give you a kung-an to meditate on. I may ask you to meditate on "What is *Wu*?" or "What is my original face?", or another classical kung-an, or I may make one up. At that point, if you are to get genuine results on this retreat, you must make finding the answer to that kung-an your life's work. Don't reflect on it, or try to reason out an answer. You'll never get it that way. You must work on it as if chewing on nails. You must use it to form in your mind a hot ball of doubt that will drive you to find the answer.

I will now give some comments on kung-ans that will help your understanding of how they are used in practice. The kung-ans that have been handed down consist of sayings, instructions, and dialogues of Ch'an masters and their students. The word "sayings" implies more than verbal communication, for sometimes the master presented a kung-an without saying anything. The recorded sayings and actions hint at, but do not directly reveal, the meaning of the kung-ans, which can only be intuited by direct experience.

To one who does not understand their special quality, kung-ans may seem to be a dialogue between insane, or at the very least, eccentric people. Generally, the kung-ans which are most clear are the most shallow, while the ones which are most obscure are the deepest. In fact, the different classes of kung-ans reflect the different levels of enlightenment.

Can a disciple discern the levels of enlightenment, and will his Shih-fu know when he or she has gone deeper? Certainly, if a student has made some genuine progress, the feeling will be very distinct. It's as distinct as the difference between night and day. The student should know if he or she has made a genuine step. Of course, his Shih-fu should be able to tell also. Otherwise he is not a very good master. Furthermore, someone who has had deep experiences can usually tell that one kung-an belongs to a certain level and another to a different level. Even within the same kung-an, the phrases and sentences may reveal different levels of meaning.

One who has worked hard enough to get to the door of Ch'an knows not what he eats, can't see what's before him, hears nothing, needs no sleep. Until he enters, this stage is called "ignoring reality." After he enters the door for the first time, he returns to a more normal mental state. Any feelings of pride or inferiority he had before will be greatly diminished.

In one kung-an the question is asked: "What are nuns?" And the answer given is "Nuns are women." This is a common sense, straightforward answer. If it comes from an average person there's nothing special about it, but if it comes from one who has practiced very hard and entered the door of Ch'an, then it actually indicates some level of enlightenment, although it is not necessarily a deep level of enlightenment. One student, after a lot of hard work, finally got through the door. I asked her, "Where are you?" She answered, "I am here." "What are you sitting on?" "I'm sitting on a chair." This is not deep enlightenment, but she has entered the door of Ch'an. She has gone from "ignoring reality" to a more normal state.

I gave a kung-an to another student, and said, "If you give me the same answer you gave me last year, I'll give you a sharp tap with the incense staff." Last year, I held up the incense staff and asked her, "What is this?" She answered, "An incense staff." This year, sure enough, she gave me the same answer, so I scolded her. At the next interview, I held up the incense staff again, and asked, "What is this?" This time she was hesitant and afraid. She thought for a while and said, "It's Buddha-nature." Hearing this, I gave her a sharp tap with the staff.

Common sense says it is an incense staff. From that point of view she was correct the first time. From the Buddhist point of view, to say it is Buddha-nature is also correct. However, her answers did not come spontaneously from her practice, so she deserved a scolding.

Another student, after working hard for a few days, came in for an interview. I picked up a wild flower and asked him, "What is this?" He answered, "A flower." "What color is it?" "Yellow." I scolded him, and he became very resentful, saying that it was indeed a yellow flower. So I tapped him sharply, and said, "This is neither a flower nor yellow." After working hard for another day and a half without sleep, he came in for another interview. This time I held up a dry twig. He took the twig from me then handed it back, saying, "I have nothing to say." I said, "Make three prostrations," thus indicating to him that he had achieved a level of comprehension.

These are living kung-ans, as distinct from the classical sayings that have been handed down. Some may understand the meaning behind the actions. To others they may just appear crazy and nonsensical. However, a student should not hope that he can pretend to be crazy and get my approval. There's really no way to pretend. If you try to, as soon as you come in, I'll chase you out. A while back a student came to see me. Looking me boldly in the eye, he said, "Test me." Again, I just looked at him and he lowered his head. I told him, "You have courage but you're lazy. You'll have to work a lot harder to enter the door."

In the previous kung-an I told that student that a yellow flower was neither a flower nor yellow. In this respect I am not a very good Shih-fu because, having said this, I saved him years of hard work. Afterwards I asked him, "Was it easy for you to enter the door?" He answered, "No." "Would it have been possible without Shih-fu?" "Impossible." Actually I have been generous to students, giving them hints and guidelines to help them enter the door quickly, to give them some small taste of Ch'an. The levels these students have reached, however, are actually very shallow. Therefore, I constantly remind them of this and warn them against pride. Even though their faith is established, they will regress unless they continue to practice hard.

On the sixth day of a retreat I gave another student a hint which actually was taken from a remark by a Reverend Jih-Ch'ang, who was helping me with the retreat: "An egg and a rock knocked against each other; the rock was broken and the egg remained whole." Unfortunately, the student was unable to make use of this hint to reach a deeper level. Another example of this type of kung-an is: "A man is walking on a bridge; the bridge flows but the water is still." This type is somewhat puzzling, but if we were to go up another level, the kung-ans would again become very normal.

So the practice on retreat should proceed as follows. You begin at the normal, everyday level. After working hard you enter a stage where everything suddenly becomes abnormal. Then, after a life and death struggle, you enter the door of Ch'an and again see everything as normal. But don't be misled; this "normal" is quite different from the "normal" of the man on the street. At this point your mind is quite clear, but you should press onward until you reach a higher abnormal stage. Kung-ans such as "Where am I?" represent the normal stage just after entering the door, whereas the "egg and the rock" type of kung-an represents the second abnormal stage. This is followed by still deeper abnormal stages. Ch'an masters have used various ways to chart the stages of progress one should pass through. Some speak of passing three major barriers, others set up four stages, but these are just rough classifications. Generally speaking, a person will go through tens or even hundreds of changes from abnormal to normal, from negation to affirmation, before reaching perfection. If you want to accomplish this in one lifetime, you must genuinely practice very hard every moment.

How can practicing Ch'an change your perceptions and attitudes? It can by using great pressure to uncover and completely utilize your hidden mental power. It's like physical power. We know we have a lot of hidden physical power which can be used in extreme situations. For example, a person being chased by a tiger may suddenly find the strength to run faster than he normally could. Things like this happen. You don't know where the strength comes from, but you somehow find it when you need it. Similarly, Ch'an is a method for putting a student in a desperate mental situation, forcing him to use his hidden power to save himself.

To reach this stage, you must first attain a certain degree of concentration. Without it, you can't even begin to practice Ch'an. Then you must advance to a samadhi-like stage, which we call "meditation." When your mind is powerfully concentrated, and free of stray thoughts, you are ready to *t'san ch'an* (investigate Ch'an), to practice kung-an.

The spirit of kung-an is that mind and Dharma are one. What is Dharma? Dharma is what the Buddha experienced when he became fully enlightened. It cannot be described. It is everywhere; it is everything. Mind and Dharma must be in harmony to generate the power leading to enlightenment. The kung-ans may seem absurd, but their underlying meanings correspond to the Dharma, issue from Dharma, because the master's mind is one with Dharma. This is why it is so important to have a Shih-fu, a teacher, who represents the living Dharma. On retreat, I tell my students to prostrate to their Shih-fu in gratitude. I then ask them, "Are you prostrating to Sheng-yen or to Shih-fu? They reply, "To Shih-fu." There is nothing special about Sheng-yen. It is only in his role as Shih-fu that he represents the Dharma. When Dharma, Shih-fu, and student are harmonized, the student becomes enlightened.

The Experience of Wu

The door of Ch'an is entered by *Wu*. When we meditate on *Wu* we ask "What is *Wu*?" On entering *Wu*, we experience emptiness; we are not aware of existence, either our or the world's. This is an elementary level of *Wu*; if it is enlightenment, it is shallow enlightenment. When we go deeper, everything exists again. We discover that the mind reflects everything. This is a deep level of *Wu*.

In to enlightenment, there is emptiness. Out of enlightenment, there is existence. These phrases are not easy to understand. When we enter *Wu*, what are we seeking? Nothing. Nothing can be pursued or sought. Thus it is *Wu*, "nothing" or "there is not." But when one is deeply enlightened, what happens? At that time, there is nothing in life that confuses, misleads, or poses any problem. One is as expansive as time and space. Thus we say that entering the realm of *Wu*, there is emptiness; going deeper into *Wu*, one returns to existence. Emptiness and existence are not two separate things. They are just one thing. Fundamentally, *Wu* is the same as existence. If there is existence in deep enlightenment, is there also self?

Yes. If you didn't have a self, you wouldn't be able to do anything. In truth, it is the attachment to self that has vanished.

Therefore, you should not think that the self ceases to exist with enlightenment. The enlightened self exists on behalf of all things. However, at the deepest levels of enlightenment one does not exist on behalf of anything; one just exists.

In Buddhism we often speak of the enlightened state as "no-self" because we have no better words for it. What this phrase says is that, at this stage, existence does not rely on self, others, or anything. It is a spontaneous, natural existence. Accordingly, one helps sentient beings. Not for the sake of self, not for the sake of others; one just naturally helps sentient beings.

Deeply enlightened persons need not maintain any particular identity; they have no need for position or place. Nor is it necessary for them to adopt an identity in accordance with the sentient beings they are helping. Bodhisattvas have no particular point of view. Like a mirror, they are only a reflection of sentient beings. They do not say, "I will behave in this or that way to help people." They reflect the problems and attitudes of sentient beings, but fundamentally these problems don't exist for them. Otherwise, they would need a point of view. When one exists neither for oneself nor for others, but just naturally helps sentient beings, this is called "no function." If you were to have a particular point of view, then it wouldn't be "no function." When you think of function, you're still thinking in terms of "in order to . . ." So we say "no function." This is *Wu*, emptiness.

The Stages of Enlightenment

It is very difficult to speak of enlightenment with detail or precision. Buddhists, Christians, Hindus, Taoists, Sufis, and Jewish mystics all describe enlightenment experiences. Are all such experiences the same? So long as you practice sincerely, regardless of the path, any experience which gives you a more profound view of life, and which has a powerfully positive effect on your character, can be called "enlightenment." But these experiences differ in their depth, and in this sense they cannot be said to be exactly the same. Even the same person will experience different levels of enlightenment at different times.

In Buddhism there are nine levels of samadhi. The first level is not true samadhi but rather a pre-samadhi stage. At this level you are clearly aware of the environment, yet you are not aware of your own existence. There is simply no separation between yourself and the world. There is no sense of big or small, external or internal, good or evil. Your mind is completely relaxed and in a state of delight. You feel no suffering, no tension, no vexation. Although this is only the pre-samadhi stage, it is a very good experience. Some people already call this stage "enlightenment" and there is nothing wrong with this.

One level higher than pre-samadhi is initial samadhi. This is the first stage that is considered genuine samadhi. In this stage there is a very cool expansive feeling accompanied by radiant light and beautiful sounds. You feel that time and space do not exist. People who reach this level are attached to meditation because they desire this "joy of samadhi." It would be very difficult for them to obey a command not to meditate. Many people would also be tempted to call this initial samadhi stage "enlightenment." However, from the Buddhist point of view this is not genuine enlightenment, at least, not deep enlightenment. But if people want to call it enlightenment, again, there is nothing seriously wrong with it.

I have just described the first of eight levels of genuine samadhi, which is called "the stage when samadhi arises and you feel happiness and contentment." I will not go into the other seven levels now. But it is important to know that there are many levels of samadhi. In fact, even the experience of pre-samadhi would be of great help to us in life. So it is quite all right for people who have been dramatically changed by these experiences to call it enlightenment. I do not want to negate their significance. I just want to emphasize to the serious practitioner that this is just the beginning.

Is it possible to say what genuine enlightenment is? Indeed, if Sakyamuni Buddha described himself as enlightened then he would not really be a Buddha, because a Buddha would not have such a thought. Actually, Sakyamuni only claimed to have found a way for sentient beings to liberate themselves from suffering. Besides, any description of enlightenment would be inadequate since it would use language, and enlightenment transcends language. Finally, it can even be said that there is really no such thing as genuine enlightenment, only various kinds of experiences that seem to correspond more or less to an ideal. Nevertheless, we refer to it because in teaching the Dharma, it seems to be necessary. We have to point to a goal even if we can't describe it.

How do you establish a real foundation that can lead to enlightenment? Very simply, you must start from the beginning and go through a process of training and practice. After a long while this may culminate in what can be called "gradual enlightenment." When you finally reach that point, however, that single dramatic event can be considered "sudden enlightenment." It's like going on a trip; you have to take the first step before you can reach your goal. But after many steps, suddenly you are there. There's no reaching a distant goal without taking many steps. In this sense there is no such thing as sudden enlightenment, if by that is meant leaping right into it with no work or preparation. Nevertheless there have been many who had no prior practice, yet were enlightened very quickly. Others practice for a whole lifetime without results. Why is this?

When enlightenment comes very quickly, we call it "sudden enlightenment"; when it takes a long time, we call it "gradual enlightenment." We say that people who get enlightened quickly have "sharp karmic roots," and people who do not, have "dull karmic roots." Where do these distinctions between sudden and gradual, sharp and dull come from? In Buddhism we believe that the time span of a life includes one's past as well as future lives. When we meet someone with sharp karmic roots, we believe that they must have practiced diligently in past lives to have such good karma. Such people have a good chance of becoming enlightened in this life, or some life in the near future. Conversely, we believe that people of dull karmic roots did not practice too well in prior lives, but may sharpen their karmic roots by being diligent now. Taking into account that a person's history spans many lives, we can see there is really no difference between sudden and gradual enlightenment, or sharp and dull karmic roots. It is a very gradual process which sometimes ripens very quickly, in a flash of joyous awakening. So, as Buddhists, we believe that the fruition of practice depends on how diligently one has practiced in both the past and the present.

The important thing is whether people believe in rebirth. This belief is often difficult to accept in its entirety even among practicing Buddhists. But those who do not believe in rebirth have no way of explaining the differences in people's achievements in the practice. They can merely imagine that some are more fortunate than others. From the standpoint of a single life, yes, there is good and bad fortune. But from the standpoint of many lives over eons of time, the force of karma applies equally to all. This is the law of karma, of cause and effect.

There are two stories that illustrate at least two stages of enlightenment. The first appears in the Platform Sutra of the Sixth Patriarch. It goes like this:

At one time the Sixth Patriarch Hui-Neng was staying at a certain temple. Two young monks there were observing a flag on a pole. One monk said, "See how the flag moves in the wind?" The other responded, "No, the flag can't move, it is the wind that is moving." The Sixth Patriarch, overhearing this debate, said "Neither flag nor wind moves. Mind is moving." Upon hearing this, the two monks realized his meaning.

The first monk's comment that the flag was moving is a simplistic observation. The second monk, who said that the wind was moving, at least had some scientific knowledge. But the Sixth Patriarch tried to help them reach a higher stage with his remark. Earlier, I explained the pre-samadhi stage, when the mind is already stationary. The world still exists then, but you sense no distinction between yourself and the world. So it is at this stage that your mind and everything else is unmoving. The Sixth

Patriarch was in effect telling the monks they should practice harder, since their perceptions were off the mark. After experiencing the pre-samadhi state, one will realize that it is the mind that moves, not external objects.

Another version of this story appears later. After the Sixth Patriarch, there was a sect of Ch'an called *Ts'ao-tung* (*Soto* in Japanese). Ts'ao-Shan, the second patriarch of this sect, had a nun disciple, name Miao-Hsin, whose duties at the temple included taking care of the accommodations of visiting monks and nuns. Once, seventeen monks arrived from faraway Szechuan Province to pay respects to the Second Patriarch. That night the monks stayed up, talking about Ch'an and the Sixth Patriarch and, in particular, the story about the flag. They talked about flag moving, wind moving, and mind moving. The nun, who was listening, finally said, "Hah! Let's see how long you people can continue moving!" She then retired to her own quarters. Hearing this remark, the monks were very impressed. They felt that the nun's words had great significance. So they marched in single file to ask her to expound on her remark. But she only said: "All this talk about flag moving, wind moving, mind moving? There is nothing moving!" The monks were stunned. They realized that while they eagerly awaited her words, their minds were moving. So they packed up and left in the middle of the night, feeling unqualified to pay respects to the

Second Patriarch. This story indicates another level of enlightenment.

As I said, in the pre-samadhi stage the mind is not moving. However, it still exists. This means that the practitioner has not yet reached a genuinely enlightened state. The nun was saying that even if you get to a stage where the mind is not moving, you still have to move on to a stage where the mind itself does not exist. And so the monks, whose minds were still moving as they listened to the nun, realized that they were at least two stages away from genuine enlightenment.

To repeat, when the mind is not moving, that is samadhi and a good state, but not genuine enlightenment. Genuine enlightenment corresponds to the state of "no mind," and that is the same thing as "noself." The mind moving corresponds to a very narrow sense of self, or "small self." The mind not moving corresponds to a very expanded sense of self, or "large self." From the point of view of Ch'an, only the stage of "no mind" is the beginning of genuine enlightenment.

How is this "no mind" different from the stages of samadhi? There's a great difference because throughout the nine stages sensations still exist; even in the highest stage there is a sensation of nothingness – no time, no space, no thoughts. People who reach this stage may very well feel that they have attained ultimate liberation, but this very feeling shows that their mind still exists. A person who

practices well but without good guidance may reach
the ninth level of samadhi and mistake this for final
liberation. In the state of true enlightenment, however, there is no feeling of being liberated, nor is
there a feeling of being unliberated.

A Dream

In the last seven days we have been living a common dream. Now this dream is over. In the seven-day dream there were people who entered, people who left. We have had tears, we have had laughter, we have had pain. We experienced it all. Some were consoled, some were scolded; sometimes we were sad, sometimes happy.

I am very happy. When the retreat started, aside from the daily schedule, I did not have any specific plans. I just had confidence and a strong desire. In the past seven days my actions were really not mine; I was just acting out of my perception-response, just as, if you hit me, I will feel pain. So it is with everything; if you feel grateful, you need not feel grateful to Shih-fu, you should be grateful to the Three Jewels. Without the blessing and the power of the Three Jewels, we couldn't possibly have had such a successful result. I have said many times before that I do not have any super powers to know what others are thinking. I just acted with the blessing and through the power of the Three Jewels.

On the first night I had a discussion with Reverend Jih-Ch'ang regarding which ones here had good chances. However, this was soon forgotten. After that I was completely using my perception-response. To put it more clearly, the Three Jewels used my body and mouth to make this dream happen. I can really say that every moment, every second, I was concentrating on serving you and observing your progress. From the third day, I have been like a midwife, or should I say, like an anxious father outside the delivery room. Now I am completely exhausted. To see that the child was safely born, I was very happy to the point of tears. The Three Jewels have borrowed my body for seven days. That's why I feel so tired. In esoteric Buddhism, there are some specific Dharma methods. When the master transmits one of these methods to a disciple, he uses so much energy, he ends up losing some weight. Now I completely understand this. Maybe it will take quite a few weeks before I can completely recover. I didn't transmit my blood to your bodies, but my energy is in you.

I cannot control your thoughts and goals, or whether you are grateful to the Three Jewels for this experience. I only want to make one more comment. Our karmic relations weren't actually created this week. For example, there are some on whom I spent very little energy, who got much out of this retreat. Others, on whom I spent a lot of energy, did not get as much. Why? Because our karmic conditions are all different. These conditions, created in the past, came to fruition in this retreat.

If your karma was not ripe enough for progress at this time and you continue practicing, eventually it will surely ripen. If you are one of these, I want to put more effort into helping you. There is no one who cannot get enlightened. Those of you who feel that you have gotten little are getting a lot. Those of you who feel you have gotten a lot are getting very little. Regardless of how you feel, it is simply too early to be disappointed or proud. Don't be discouraged, don't be satisfied. We should all continue to work hard. Those who made good progress should work the hardest. Don't worry about where Shih-fu will be. With good causes and conditions we will be together. The retreat is over. What happens next? Think about it. Of course, if this was truly a dream, everything I just said was only nonsense. In that case, forget it.

Contemplating Mind
By Han-Shan Te-Ch'ing (1546-1623)

Look upon the body as unreal,
An image in a mirror,
Or the reflection of the moon in water.
Contemplate the mind as formless,
Yet bright and pure.
Not a single thought arising,
Empty, yet perceptive,
Still, yet illuminating,
Complete like the Great Emptiness,
Containing all that is wonderful.
Neither going out nor coming in,
Without appearance or characteristics,
Countless skillful means
Arise out of one mind.
Independent of material existence,
Which is ever an obstruction,
Do not cling to deluded thoughts.
These give birth to illusion.

Attentively contemplate this mind,
Empty, devoid of all objects.
If emotions should suddenly arise,
You will fall into confusion.
In a critical moment bring back the light,
Powerfully illuminating.
Clouds disperse, the sky is clear,
The sun shines brilliantly.
If nothing arises within the mind,
Nothing will manifest without.
That which has characteristics
Is not original reality.
If you can see a thought as it arises,
This awareness will at once destroy it.
Whatever state of mind should come,
Sweep it away, put it down.
Both good and evil states
Can be transformed by mind.
Sacred and profane appear
In accordance with thoughts.
Reciting mantras or contemplating mind
Are merely herbs for polishing a mirror.
When the dust is removed,
They are also wiped away.
Great extensive spiritual powers
Are all complete within the mind.

The Pure Land or the Heavens
Can be traveled to at will.
You need not seek the real,
Mind originally is Buddha.
The familiar becomes remote,
The strange seems familiar.
Day and night, everything is wonderful.
Nothing you encounter confuses you.
These are the essentials of mind.

On 'Contemplating Mind' By Han-Shan

Han-Shan Te-Ch'ing was one of the four great Ch'an masters who lived at the end of the Ming Dynasty. At the age of seven he already had doubts about his origin and destiny. At nine he entered a monastery, and at nineteen became a monk. His first attempts to practice Ch'an were fruitless, and he turned to reciting the Buddha's name, which brought better results. After this he resumed the practice of Ch'an with more success. While listening to the Avatamsaka Sutra, he realized that in Dharmadhatu, the realm of all phenomena, even the tiniest thing contains the whole universe. Later he read another book called *Things Not Moving*, and experienced another enlightenment. He wrote a poem which said:

Death and birth, day and night,
Water flowing, flowers withering,
It's only now I know
That nostrils point downwards.

On another day, while walking, he suddenly entered samadhi, and experienced a brilliant light like a huge, perfect mirror, with mountains and water, everything in the world reflected in it. When he returned from samadhi, his body and mind were completely clear; he realized there was nothing to attain. Then he wrote this poem:

In the flash of one thought
My turbulent mind came to rest.
The inner and the outer,
The senses and their objects,
Are thoroughly lucid.
In a complete turnabout
I smashed the Great Emptiness.
The ten thousand manifestations
Arise and disappear
Without any reason.

For many years as a wandering monk, Han-Shan studied Ch'an under several leading masters and spent long periods living in solitude in the mountains. He engaged in altruistic acts, propagated the Dharma, and lectured on sutras. He was a scholar and prolific writer, leaving behind many works on all aspects of Buddhism. He exemplified the Bodhisattva ideal of developing wisdom through meditation, study, and compassionate action. In the spirit of his times, he did not make a strong distinction between the sects of Buddhism, but was eclectic, also incorporating elements of Confucianism. His style was a fusion of the austerity of Ch'an with the inclusive view of the Hua-yen sect. To this day his undecayed body remains intact in the monastery of the Sixth Patriarch on mainland China. "Contemplating Mind" is one among many of Master Han-Shan's poems and songs which deal with the approach one should take to practice. This short *ming*, or verse, describes practice as not going beyond mind and body — that there is nothing other than mind or body that can be used as tools of practice.

> Look upon the body as unreal,
> An image in a mirror,
> Or the reflection of the moon in water.
> Contemplate the mind as formless,
> Yet bright and pure.

The poet asks us to literally look upon the body as non-existent. In Buddhist analysis, form, taken to be the physical world, is the first of the five *skandhas*, or phenomenal aggregates. These aggregates together create the illusion of existence. Form is the material component. The other four *skandhas* — sensation, perception, volition, and consciousness — are all mental components. A person who is able to contemplate the five *skandhas* well would be considered enlightened. In Buddhist analysis, the body is composed of the four elements: earth, water, fire, and wind. If we were to separate these elements, our body would not exist. These elements come together because of the force of our previous karma. A body which is thus compounded is not genuinely real. Being the result, or the reflection, of our previous karma, it is like the reflection of the moon in water. If the mind didn't create karma, then the elements would not accumulate and combine to make up the body. If we take this body, this result of previous mental karma, as real, then it's like looking upon the moon in the water as the real moon. Further, the body is in a constant state of change, and has no truly fixed existence.

If we can realize the illusory nature of the body, the mind will settle down and our vexations will clear up. All our vexations, associated with greed, hatred, and delusion, arise because we identify with the body, and want to protect it and seek benefits for it. Because of the body, we give rise to the five desires, namely, food, sex, sleep, fame, and wealth. To undo vexations, first break the attachment to the body; then break away from the view that the body is truly substantial. But this view is very difficult to break. In the sutras it is said that *sakaya*, the view of having a body, is as difficult to uproot as a mountain. So, Han-Shan tells us, once we can see the body as unreal, we can begin to work on the mind.

The practice begins by contemplating the mind as formless. Ordinarily the mind has all kinds of forms or characteristics: greed, hatred, ignorance, pride, doubt, jealousy, and selfishness. They manifest mainly because of the body. Some people might think, "Death will end my vexations since I'll no longer have a body." But after you die you still have a body, and you will still have vexations. When this body is gone, a new one begins. Where there's a body, there is vexation. If the mind had fixed characteristics, it would not be changeable, and there would be no point in practicing. But the mind is always changing. The mind of the ordinary person is characterized by vexation, and the mind of a sage is characterized by wisdom; otherwise they are the same.

> Not a single thought arising,
> Empty, yet perceptive,
> Still, yet illuminating,
> Complete like the Great Emptiness,
> Containing all that is wonderful.

The mind that is without even one thought is extremely bright and pure, but this doesn't mean that it is blank. "No thought" means no characteristics, and blankness itself is a characteristic. In this condition the mind is unmoving, yet perceives everything very clearly. Although wisdom is empty, it is not without a function. What is this function? Without moving it reflects and illuminates everything. It is like the moon shining on water. Although each spot of water reflects a different image of the moon, the moon itself remains the same. But it doesn't say, "I shine." It just shines. Great Emptiness has no limits. It gives rise neither to feelings of moving nor not moving. Nothing detracts from its purity and brightness. This is the mind of wisdom. It is the mind of the Buddhas and Bodhisattvas. It is also the ability to help sentient beings.

Neither going out nor coming in,
Without appearance or characteristics,

To practice is to cultivate the mind. If you successfully contemplate the mind, all merits and functions within the mind are at your disposal. But as soon as one thought arises, everything is obscured. If while practicing you feel your mind expanding infinitely, that feeling gives you away. If you suddenly feel, "Ah! I've discovered a limitlessly great expanse! I am liberated!" in reality you are still within the sphere of the limited. Only neither-going-nor-coming is boundless. Being boundless, it has no circumference, so there's no way to find an entrance. To think of leaving is to imagine that there could be a better place, so there is no going either.

When Master T'ai-Hsu had his first enlightenment, when he saw limitless light and sound, he felt he was in a very deep faraway state. That was still not Great Emptiness since it was not without form. In his second experience there was nothing there that could be explained or described. If there was still something he could describe, it could not be formless.

Countless skillful means
Arise out of one mind.

Skillful means, the various methods of helping oneself and others to liberation, are the bountiful yield of this practice. Liberation means going from ignorance to wisdom. The idea of *ch'iao,* translated as "mind" here, does not strictly refer to the mind of one thought. It is the original substance of infinitude. *Ch'iao* literally means a hole or cavity. In Chinese mythology, in the beginning the universe was a ball of chaos. Then a god came along and knocked a hole in it with a hammer. That caused the separation of heaven and earth, sun, and moon, etc. *Ch'iao* also has the meaning of "wisdom." To call it "mind," one would have to say it's a pure mind.

Independent of material existence,
Which is ever an obstruction,
Do not cling to deluded thoughts.
These give birth to illusion.

Like *ch'iao,* many words in this poem have a Taoist or Confucian origin. Two other examples are *hsing* and *ch'i,* literally, form and energy, translated here as "material existence." There is a saying: "What is above form is the Way, what is below form is *Ch'i.*" The closest meaning of *ch'i* would be life-energy; it moves the universe. Where there is *ch'i,* there is also form.

Although *chi* is invisible, we see its effects, just as we see the wind in the swaying branches of a tree. "Material existence" includes all forms and energy, both visible and invisible. Wherever there is energy and form, there is also obstruction. So please do not rely on material existence to overcome delusion — it is the cause of delusion.

What are deluded thoughts? When meditating are you aware of wandering thoughts? Hopefully you are. But in daily life do you actually believe in your experiences, your plans, your abilities, your knowledge? They are just a series of more or less connected delusions. If you act on delusions, all kinds of strange things may occur. (The word translated here as "illusion" means that which is weird or strange.) The more firmly you believe in them, the more likely they are to arise.

Delusions are usually created by the five desires. To fulfill the demands of the five desires, people seek the satisfactions of material things, and of the flesh. In the end, are you really satisfied? After eating a meal, are you satisfied? Of course you are, for the moment. But a few hours later your craving for food begins anew. It's an endless cycle; not only are you concerned about getting food now, but this worry follows you into old age. Truly there is no end to desire.

Attentively contemplate this mind,
Empty, devoid of all objects.

If emotions should suddenly arise,
You will fall into confusion.

If we contemplate the mind well, we discover there is nothing in it. If there is something in it, such as an emotion, then there is still attachment. It is only necessary for you to give rise to a momentary or sudden emotion to set your mind in motion.

In a critical moment bring back the light,
Powerfully illuminating.

When you find yourself muddled, you should realize it right away and tell yourself, "This is false, an attachment." In this manner, your wisdom will come into play and grow in power. The difficulty is that you may not always recognize your confused state. According to the patriarchs, you must use wisdom to shine on all your delusions. But someone in the confused state supposes what he sees is real. Therefore, he would not search for the light of wisdom. Only if he realizes his confusion, then, in a critical moment, can he turn around.

Clouds disperse, the sky is clear,
The sun shines brilliantly.

Realizing your delusion, if through practice you could illuminate the mind that is originally empty, it would be like the sky after dark clouds have dispersed. Sometimes while practicing you seem to have no thoughts; still, your mind is not really clear. This would be like a hot, hazy day when vapor rises and obscures the sun. Sometimes, after a few days of retreat, I ask people how close they think they are to enlightenment. Some say, "Well, it seems like it's right around the corner, but I can't see it." Sometimes around the edges of a dark cloud we can see rays of sunlight, so we know that the sun is there. Only by seeing it yourself will you know that a brilliant sun shines behind the cloud. Those who have seen some rays of light will become firm in their faith and will practice harder.

> If nothing arises within the mind,
> Nothing will manifest without.
> That which has characteristics
> Is not original reality.

If no thoughts arise, nothing will be experienced outside of the mind. If you think that something is manifesting without, it is an illusion. In the Platform Sutra it says that neither the flag nor the wind moves. It is the mind that moves. When the mind is still, there is nothing outside that can tempt or disturb you. Do the thoughts that disturb you come from outside or inside? If only inside thoughts bother you, then you are practicing well. But even getting to this point is not easy.

Feelings that relate to our own body, such as hunger, heat, cold, or pain, are really outer things. Other thoughts may arise that originate in the mind. For example, I may say to people, "Tell me when the body and the method disappear and I'll give you a new method." So during their sitting, they may think, "Strange. How is it that my body is still here? Body, go quickly! Get lost! I want a new method." Then when the body finally disappears, they think, "What's this? How come the method is still here? When will it disappear? Shih-fu told us about infinite light and sound. Why haven't I experienced that yet? Maybe it's coming soon. But why can't I get anywhere? Ah! Shih-fu told us not to think like this. Better not force anything. He tells us not to think of enlightenment. OK. I won't think of it, I'll just practice. This time, I won't be afraid of dying. But it seems like I can't die. Why?"

These conversations with yourself while meditating are not related to the body or the outer environment; they originate in the mind. These are meaningless delusions, mental chaos. How do you get rid of this chaos? Very simple. As soon as a thought comes up, just ignore it and go back to the method. Whether it originates in your mind or in the environment, it lacks reality. Some people may say, "I know I am confused, but I can't do anything about it." That is why practice is needed — to help those who at least recognize their confusion to do something about it.

> *If you can see a thought as it arises,*
> *This awareness will at once destroy it.*
> *Whatever state of mind should come,*
> *Sweep it away, put it down.*

There is a saying about the practice: "Don't be afraid of a thought arising, just be afraid of noticing it too late." It's not such a terrible thing for thoughts to arise. The problem is when you're not aware of them. If you realize it as soon as a thought arises, then it doesn't matter. It will help you to work harder. If there were no thoughts arising at all, you would already have a pure mind and you wouldn't need to practice. People who have never practiced may know about their wandering thoughts, but can do nothing to stop them.

When you are practicing hard, whatever thought comes up you have the power to just sweep it away. To sweep means to ignore, not to dislike, or to resist the thought. How else could you sweep it away? If you resist it with something else, that something else is also a thought. If I wanted to get rid of Tom and got Dick to do the job, after Tom left I would still be stuck with Dick. No matter how many people I find to get the other one out, there would always be one left. If you get involved with feelings after the thought is already gone, thinking, "What bad luck. I hope it doesn't come up again," your mind will be scattered. Then you begin to think, "I'm hopelessly sunk in wandering thoughts. I'll just give up meditating." If you practice this way, the wandering thoughts don't get swept away, they just accumulate. This is because you haven't put down the state of mind which gave rise to the thoughts in the first place.

Or are you the type who tries to grab the wandering thought and say to it, "I'm not going to let you come again"? Actually, if you are really able to grab hold of it, at least you have the intention of watching it. If you were to continue watching that thought, then that very state of mind would become your method. Is that possible? Some people start to work on "What is *Wu*?" and it eventually becomes "What am I?" Then they even forget that and they are working on "I, I, I." One student started working on "What is *Wu*?" and ended up by asking "Where is my heart?" I told him that wasn't the right question, he should be working on *Wu*. But he kept on looking all over for his heart. Finally he picked up a feather outside and said, "Oh! Here's where my heart is!" If you can take a wandering thought and just fix onto it without letting go, this in itself becomes a method. If you can't hold onto it, then any thought, good or bad, is a delusion that disturbs your practice. The most important thing is, whatever is past, just let it go. Your mind should be like a mirror, not a camera. Whatever goes into a camera is recorded there; the reflection in a mirror vanishes when the object moves away.

Both good and evil states
Can be transformed by mind.
Sacred and profane appear
In accordance with thoughts.

Everything is a product of your mind. If the mind didn't move, no discriminations would be made. According to your situation you will see certain things as good or bad. But this is always changing, and the things themselves don't have any of these fixed characteristics. There is no definite standard of good and evil; it all depends on your viewpoint at the moment.

The state of a person's mind makes him perceive some people as common, others as holy. To some people Jesus was really an evil person who ought to be killed. To his disciples, he was a saint. One student, after she worked very hard on a retreat, said she saw a light emanating from my body. So she knelt down, taking me for a holy man. Later on, when she discontinued practicing Ch'an, she just saw me as a common person again. According to Buddha Dharma, saintliness or ordinariness are in the mind of the beholder. Even the saintliness of such people as the Buddha or Jesus are value judgments.

When the Buddha looks at sentient beings, all sentient beings are just Buddha. When sentient beings look at the Buddha, what do you think they see? When Sakyamuni Buddha walked through the forests, or on the banks of the Ganges, do you think all the birds, ants, and other little animals saw a Buddha? If you were living at that time and had never heard of this person, Sakyamuni, when you saw him, would you think he was the Buddha, or just another wandering ascetic?

When we perceive something, that is only our idea of what exists. If I looked around this room without making discriminations of any kind, what would I see? Nine people? One person? In reality I would see not even one. If I see even one, my mind has attached to form. Understand?

Reciting mantras or contemplating mind
Are merely herbs for polishing a mirror.
When the dust is removed,
They are also wiped away.

Methods of cultivation are useful for those who are in the course of training. For those people who have reached the stage of no thought, who have completed the course of practice, methods are not needed. Some people ask themselves when they are working well, "Am I still working on the method? Where did the method go?" Originally they were working well, but this kind of thought ruins their concentration. It is like a pair of glasses that fit so naturally on you that you somehow forget you are wearing them and start looking for them. When you are working well on your method, forget that you are using a method. When you cross a bridge, once you get to the other side you wouldn't say, "Where did the bridge go?" The method is just a tool to get to your destination. Once you have arrived, it is of no further use to you.

> *Great extensive spiritual powers*
> *Are all complete within the mind.*

Some people are always looking for someone to give them some kind of psychic power, or trying to get some other benefit from someone with power. One student thought that I could give people power to make them progress more quickly, and that I could obstruct others from making progress. In the beginning he had some benefit from the practice and felt I was a very good master. Sometime later, when he didn't have much success, he felt that I was obstructing him with some magic spell. Another person told me that a Zen master used spiritual power to ruin his family life and unsettle his mind. He asked me to give him some power to combat the other master. I told him, "That person is a Ch'an master, and according to the spirit of Ch'an, he would not do something like that." But he said, "No, he really does have this power. If I don't go to his place, then my problems begin." So I said, "Then you should go regularly." Actually, none of this was happening. It was all in his mind.

We call this "practicing outer paths" because your faith is not in yourself but only in outer things. The usual interpretation of the Chinese term *wai tao* is "outside of Buddhist belief," that is, heretical. But the real meaning of outer paths is seeking salvation outside oneself, such as another person, a god, or even a Buddha. As such, some Buddhists may be following outer paths. Your fate is your own, relying on somebody else is foolish.

People have the potential for great spiritual power. We find it in all religions. But these powers should not be used arbitrarily. Not that the power is not available, but you wouldn't get very far with it because it cannot undo the power of people's karma. Most Ch'an masters have a certain degree of spiritual power but have a policy of not using them. I myself claim no psychic powers, but I do have a kind of perception-response, or sensitivity to situations. But the kind of perception-response I have depends on the situation at the moment. Because spiritual powers are not reliable and are dangerous to use, I have never sought them. People may like it as a novelty, but after a while they get bored. Such supernatural powers can only stimulate or excite; they don't give people a lasting sense of security. To my mind these things are of no use.

Another kind of spiritual power is using the power of our minds to communicate, to set up karmic affinities, with sentient beings. For example, wise people or religious leaders may give a lecture that moved people to become converted on the spot. In this sense, Jesus, Sakyamuni, and Confucius are all people with great spiritual powers. In contrast, the biggest recorded audience that ever attended the lectures of the Great Master Ou-I of the Ming dynasty was fourteen people. But this master has had a great influence on Chinese Buddhism. So the best kind of spiritual power is that which benefits people down through the ages, not just a cheap thrill or excitement. Your own mind is the source of all the power you need.

> *The Pure Land or the Heavens*
> *Can be traveled to at will.*

If your mind is pure, then wherever you are will also be pure. If you have a heavenly mind, then you are in heaven. If you're feeling very miserable, you're in hell. But the sad thing is, most people can so freely go to hell, but not so freely to heaven. If I were to grab you right now and give you a good scolding, and you said, "I didn't do anything wrong. What are you yelling at me for?" At that time your mind would be full of misery and vexations. You would be in hell. But if, when I scolded and whacked you, you were to turn around, bow deeply, with tears running down your cheeks, and say, "I am so grateful for the chance to burn up some of my great karmic obstruction," you would be in heaven. But to have a mind like that is rather rare. So these two lines at first glance look strange, but the Pure Land, the Heavens, can all be experienced right here in the ordinary world.

You need not seek the real,
Mind is originally Buddha.

There is no such thing as the real mind. Ridding yourself of delusion: that's the real mind. There is also no Buddha. Your own mind is originally Buddha. If the mind is pure, even the Buddha isn't there. When you have no thought of becoming a Buddha, when there is no Buddha and no vexations, that is the real Buddha-mind.

The familiar becomes remote,
The strange seems familiar.
Day and night, everything seems wonderful.
Nothing you encounter confuses you.
These are the essentials of mind.

When the familiar becomes remote you look upon your family as strangers, and upon strangers as dear, close kin. Only a person with true practice can do this. But if you haven't practiced deeply and consider your parents as outsiders, without also considering outsiders as your parents, you're off the mark. When your practice becomes very deep, you will see all sentient beings as your parents. This is because your fortuitous birth as a human being was the result of many eons of cause and effect, involving untold numbers of sentient beings. Knowing this, you feel a deep sense of gratitude towards everyone and everything. Others have done much for you, and you want to express your gratitude.

But you only have one body. How can you help all sentient beings as if they were your own parents? Don't burden yourself with such thoughts. Day and night, keep your mind on the one thought of working hard. If, moment by moment, you can keep your mind in a clear state, then nothing will confuse you, and you will be able to express your gratitude freely, naturally, without obstruction.

We have talked about the poem "Contemplating Mind," which describes the general situation of the mind, and Han-Shan's explanation of practice and enlightenment. This talk is based on my own experience, making use of the poem to guide you in your practice.

Silent Illumination
By Hung-Chih Cheng-Chueh
(1091-1157)

Silently and serenely, one forgets all words,
Clearly and vividly, it appears before you.
When one realizes it, time has no limits.
When experienced, your surroundings come to life.
Singularly illuminating is this bright awareness,
Full of wonder is the pure illumination.
The moon's appearance, a river of stars,
Snow-clad pines, clouds hovering on mountain peaks.
In darkness, they glow with brightness.
In shadows, they shine with a splendid light.
Like the dreaming of a crane flying in empty space,
Like the clear, still water of an autumn pool,
Endless eons dissolve into nothingness,
Each indistinguishable from the other.
In this illumination all striving is forgotten.
Where does this wonder exist?
Brightness and clarity dispel confusion
On the path of Silent Illumination,

The origin of the infinitesimal.
To penetrate the extremely small,
There is the gold shuttle on a loom of jade.
Subject and object influence each other.
Light and darkness are mutually dependent.
There is neither mind nor world to rely on,
Yet do the two interact, mutually.
Drink the medicine of correct views.
Beat the poison-smeared drum.
When silence and illumination are complete
Killing and bringing to life are choices I make.
At last, through the door, one emerges.
The fruit has ripened on the branch.
Only this Silence is the ultimate teaching.
Only this Illumination, the universal response.
The response is without effort.
The teaching, not heard with the ears.
Throughout the universe all things,
Emit light and speak the Dharma.
They testify to each other,
Answering each other's questions.
Mutually answering and testifying,
Responding in perfect harmony.
When illumination is without serenity,
Then will distinctions be seen.
Mutually testifying and answering,

Giving rise to disharmony.
If within serenity illumination is lost,
All will become wasteful and secondary.
When Silent Illumination is complete,
The lotus will blossom, the dreamer will awaken.
The hundred rivers flow to the ocean,
The thousand mountains face the loftiest peak.
Like the goose preferring milk to water,
Like a busy bee gathering pollen,
When Silent Illumination reaches the ultimate,
I carry on the original tradition of my sect.
This practice is called Silent Illumination.
It penetrates from the deepest to the highest.

On 'Silent Illumination' By Hung-Chih

The style of meditation called "Silent Illumination" is one of the great practices of the Ch'an tradition. Silent Illumination originated around the 11th century, and its greatest advocate was Master Hung-Chih Cheng-Chueh of the Ts'ao-tung sect, which became the Soto sect in Japan. In Tibet, the *mahamudra* practice is very similar. The practice originated in India, where it was called *samatha-vipasyana*, or serenity-insight. The aim of this practice is a mind unburdened with thoughts. This leads the mind to profound awareness about its own state.

Silently and serenely one forgets all words,
Clearly and vividly it appears before you.

First there is silence, then comes illumination. Ordinarily people express themselves through a never-ending succession of words and images. This is moving away from serenity. On retreat we have the rule of no talking. Even so, is your mind ever without thoughts or words? In interviews, people tell me that their biggest problem is that they can't stop thinking. Even when you're sitting there, wordless and silent, you may be conversing with mental objects all the time. After fast-walking meditation today, I asked you to relax and put down all thoughts. Had you been able to do this, you would have achieved a state of silence and serenity, and you would be practicing at an advanced level.

Silent Illumination is a very peaceful style of meditation in which there is not one thought, yet your mind is extremely clear. I use three phrases to describe this state: first, "bright and open"; second, "no scattered thoughts"; and third, "not one thought."

When the mind drops all use of words, it becomes bright and open; this is the first characteristic. Next, "no scattered thoughts" refers to single-mindedness — total concentration on the method. But when you finally forget the method itself, and not one thought remains, that is genuine serenity. Ultimately, Silent Illumination is the method of no method. Counting and following the breath are methods of collecting the scattered mind, and kung-an is the method of applying great pressure to achieve a sudden break-through. Silent Illumination is just dropping all thoughts and words and going directly to the state of Ch'an.

I do not recommend this method to people too often. First, you must have a firm practice to really benefit from it; you must be at a stage where there's no problem becoming settled, when you can sit with unbroken concentration, with almost no outside thoughts. The other reason is that it is hard to tell whether your mind is truly "bright and open," or just blank. You can just be idling, having very subtle thoughts, and believe you are practicing Silent Illumination. You can be silent without illuminating anything.

The key is in the line, "Clearly and vividly it appears before you." What are you to be clear and vivid about? About everything in your mind, which, though motionless, reflects everything, like a mirror.

When one realizes it, time has no limits.
When experienced, your surroundings come to life.

When silence is achieved, time has no duration. It is only because thoughts come and go that we are aware of time. When there are no thoughts, neither is there time. Time is limitless, beyond measure. One night, when Great Master T'ai-Hsu was meditating he heard the evening bells. Immediately afterwards, he heard the morning bells. Because he was in samadhi, a whole night had passed during which he had no sense of time.

The next line refers to space, a clear and vivid sense of the environment. When your mind is moving, your awareness is narrowly focused by your thoughts. If you could see and hear without using your mind, and be very attentive at the same time, you would sense limitless space. But this is not an especially high state. Higher yet is the state of "not one thought." In this state distinctions of vast or small just don't exist.

There is a saying that all the Buddhas of the past, present, and future are turning the Dharma Wheel on the point of a fine hair. When you can empty your mind of all thoughts, the mind becomes all-inclusive and sees no difference between the infinitesimally small and the infinitely large.

Singularly illuminating is this bright awareness,
Full of wonder is the pure illumination.

The bright awareness that illuminates is that of a Buddha who sees sentient beings in their perfection, unlike ordinary awareness which is confused, and sees the world as dark. This brightness throws its light on all things, and they take on the aspect of wonder. This is like the songs of Milarepa, which reveal the harmony between all things great and small. It is the wonder of the Avatamsaka Sutra, where everything is seen in such detail, from every point of view. A mind so illuminated could see the cosmos in a grain of sand. This is the realm perceived by wisdom arising from samadhi.

The moon's appearance, a river of stars,
Snow-clad pines, clouds hovering on mountain peaks.

The state of Silent Illumination is like the moon unobscured by clouds — clear, soft, and cool. The moon rather than the sun symbolizes enlightenment, because the moon is cool and serene, while the sun is hot and active. "A river of stars" refers to the Milky Way where the dense stars form a river of light. "Snow-clad pines . . ." All these are images of brightness and openness.

Have you ever seen clouds move freely through upthrusting mountain peaks? This symbolizes the liberated mind which, even when it encounters obstructions, is not bound by them.

In darkness, they glow with brightness.
In shadows, they shine with a splendid light.

These lines contrast the mind of wisdom which shines even in the dark in the midst of vexation, and the mind of foolishness which remains in the dark. Wise persons, although perhaps appearing foolish, prefer obscurity. Yet they express their power in everything they do.

Like the dreaming of a crane flying in empty space,
Like the clear, still water of an autumn pool,
Endless eons dissolve into nothingness,
Each indistinguishable from the other.

The mind of Silent Illumination is broad, high, and deep. It is like the crane in flight, feeling the vastness of empty space, unaware of its own existence, silently floating in a timeless dream. The autumn pool, despite its great depth, is so still that the bottom is clearly seen. In autumn the pool is not thriving with life as it is in summer. The active elements have settled, and with settling there comes a clarity, and the depths can finally be seen.

Into the sky of the crane's dream and the depths of the autumn pool, eons of time dissolve into nothing. We term it "nothing" because our sense of time comes from the endless succession of thoughts and images passing through our minds. This flow of experience also gives rise to a sense of a separate self. If you could cease the march of thoughts through your mind, and fix on just one constant thought of Silent Illumination, time would freeze. If you could then forget even that thought, time would dissolve.

Can you fix your mind on one thought for even a minute? Is it dangerous to stop a plane in midair? Of course. But you must be determined to stop your thoughts, and not be afraid of dying. If you panic, you will be filled with thoughts. You must more than ever drop everything and concentrate on just the practice, abandoning all thoughts of life, body, fears, desires, everything but the method.

In this illumination all striving is forgotten.
Where does this wonder exist?

There are many wonders to discover in Silent Illumination. But the mind of practice cannot be the seeking mind, even if the goal is enlightenment. For while thoughts exist they are obstacles. "All striving is forgotten" means that nothing exists except illumination itself; there is no thought of losing or gaining anything. The wonder is in abandoning confusion and with a clear, bright mind, just dedicating yourself to practice.

Brightness and clarity dispel confusion
On the path of Silent Illumination,
The origin of the infinitesimal.

When we are practicing the method, vexation and ignorance diminish, wisdom and compassion increase. When vexation and ignorance reach the extreme of smallness, they vanish; when wisdom and compassion reach the extreme of largeness, they too vanish. Therefore, for all sentient beings, Bodhisattvas, and Buddhas, the path aims at lessening vexation and increasing wisdom. But at the stage of Buddhahood, neither vexation nor wisdom exist.

To penetrate the extremely small,
There is the gold shuttle on a loom of jade.

The gold shuttle and jade loom are used to weave the clothing of the devas, or heavenly beings, and symbolize the wisdom which harmonizes the realms of existence. With wisdom, the nature of the least of things can be directly perceived.

Subject and object influence each other.
Light and darkness are mutually dependent.

These lines refute the dualisms of ordinary thinking. Subject and object are mutually dependent, like light and darkness. Silent Illumination dispels the idea that wisdom is simply the absence of vexation. During this retreat, one student came to me in a very emotional state, saying that her compassion had been moved powerfully, that she felt pity for suffering people and wanted to help them. From her point of view this seemed like a very good experience to have, but I scolded her, saying, "You're just fooling around in sentimentality. This is not wisdom. In the mind of wisdom, there is no such thing as people needing to be pitied." Compassion is not simple sentimentality; it is just a natural response to help people.

There is neither mind nor world to rely on,
Yet do the two interact, mutually.

When the distinction between self and others is dropped, when there is no sense of self or outside world, inner and outer become one, and even that one will disappear. When you are practicing poorly, you can't even connect two successive thoughts, much less dissolve the boundary between inner and outer.

The previous lines describe the serene, internal aspect of Silent Illumination. The following lines deal with functioning in the world.

Drink the medicine of correct views.
Beat the poison-smeared drum.

To drink the medicine of correct views is to infuse yourself with the Dharma; to beat the poison-smeared drum is to help sentient beings kill delusion and vexation. (In Indian mythology, a drum smeared with a certain poison could kill enemies who hear the drum, even from a great distance.) Yet, while compassion and helping exist, there is no sense of saving sentient beings. You must rely on three pillars of practice – precepts, samadhi, and wisdom. Of these, samadhi produces concrete results the most easily. Someone who has had their self-centered point of view demolished even for a short time can understand Silent Illumination. But ultimately the essence of this practice is simply to sit, just sit, and keep on sitting. It is like letting the impurities in a murky pond settle until the water is so clear you can see to the bottom.

When Silence and Illumination are complete,
Killing and bringing to life are choices I make.

The spirit of the Bodhisattva is this: the path of delivering oneself from suffering lies in relieving the suffering of others. Even with this ideal, if your practice is weak, your most sincere actions cannot help. But when your practice reaches the level described in this poem, your power to help flows spontaneously, even in ways that seem unconventional. "Killing and bringing to life" means that the Bodhisattva applies any skillful means, even increasing a disciple's vexation, to bring him to realization. We kill vexations to give life to wisdom; we give life to vexations to exercise wisdom.

At last, through the door, one emerges.
The fruit has ripened on the branch.

When practice is fulfilled, the meditator passes through the door of *samsara* — the cycle of birth and death — and emerges on the path of wisdom. Having labored long and hard, his practice has ripened. The fruit of the Bodhi tree, the Buddha's tree of awakening, is ready for picking. In Ch'an practice, this "door" is described as consisting of three thresholds one must pass. The first threshold is called *ch'u ch'an*, or "initial Ch'an." By investigating Ch'an, and smashing through the wall of great doubt, you cross this threshold to see your self-nature, or Buddha nature. This is the first taste of the fruit, a glimpse of enlightenment, but not final liberation, for vexation is still deeply ingrained.

On the darkest of nights, moonless and starless, a bolt of lightning splits the sky; for an instant you see everything with stunning clarity, then darkness again. But having seen it once, your faith is increased, and you will never totally lose your practice.

The second threshold is in fact many thresholds. It is called *t'seng kuan*, the "multi-layered pass." This is like a mountain range with ever-ascending peaks, which you must pass, one by one. The peaks are your own obstructions and vexations. This stage takes a long time, but with every peak crossed, your strength grows. As vexations get lighter, the peaks seem less high.

The third and last threshold is called *lao kuan*, the "prison pass," so-called because one emerges from it into final liberation from the wheel of *samsara* — the temporal realms of past, present, and future. This liberation is called *Nirvana*. At this stage, the Bodhisattva's capacity to help sentient beings is vast and unhindered.

Only this Silence is the ultimate teaching.
Only this Illumination, the universal response.

Silence is the ultimate teaching. After a billion words are uttered, they are still not the Dharma. No description of enlightenment can approach the direct experience. Silence is itself the teaching that transcends words. Illumination is perfect wisdom. Only with perfect wisdom can you respond to all sentient beings.

The response is without effort.
The teaching, not heard with the ears.

Illumination is without effort because there is no serenity through striving. The effortless response is the way of the Bodhisattva. While others see in him great compassion, he sees himself as ordinary.

Throughout the universe all things
Emit light and speak the Dharma.

It is said that green bamboo and yellow flowers are the Buddha speaking the Dharma. But is there anything that is not a manifestation of Buddha Dharma? There is a story that Master Tao-Sheng spoke to a pile of rocks because nobody attended his lectures. According to the account, when he was finished, the rocks nodded in appreciation. But, in fact, everything is the Dharma body of the Buddha, and the illumined mind simply sees the world bright and full of vitality.

They testify to each other
Answering each other's questions.
Mutually answering and testifying,
Responding in perfect harmony.

In this conversation between all things, when everything speaks the Dharma, the response is always on the mark. The illuminated mind includes all. In it, all things are friendly and harmonious, without lack, without excess. It is a perfect conversation – the perfect answer to the perfect question; all without words.

When illumination is without serenity,
Then will distinctions be seen.
Mutually testifying and answering,
Giving rise to disharmony.

When there is illumination without silence, thoughts intrude and distinctions are made. Things lose their quality of being "just this." The dialogue between things is discordant – the wrong answers to the wrong questions.

If within serenity illumination is lost,
All will become wasteful and secondary.

In the previous lines the poet speaks of illumination without silence. Here as earlier, he speaks of silence without illumination. Neither state by itself is complete; neither is the goal of practice.

When Silent Illumination is complete,
The lotus will blossom, the dreamer will awaken.

These lines say clearly that the proper practice of Silent Illumination can lead to enlightenment. Silent Illumination is complete when serenity and illumination are both present. Much hard work and persistence are needed to get to this point. Ultimately, the Buddha lotus inherent in you will blossom, and you will awaken from the deep dream of *samsara*, the dream of vexation.

> *The hundred rivers flow to the ocean,*
> *The thousand mountains face the loftiest peak.*

The hundred rivers are like sentient beings who are attached to thinking and suffer vexations. Each river, following its own course, flows into the great ocean of wisdom where it loses its sense of self and becomes one with the ocean. The thousand mountains suggest discriminating minds which see themselves as separate, but each one ultimately gazes upon the lofty peak of wisdom, which sees only the one great mountain of all sentient beings.

> *Like the goose preferring milk to water,*
> *Like a busy bee gathering pollen,*
> *When Silent Illumination reaches the ultimate,*
> *I carry on the original tradition of my sect.*

The goose choosing nutritious milk over water and the bee busily gathering pollen are both expressing natural intelligence; you might say animal wisdom. When practicing Silent Illumination you are doing the same, completing the natural process of attaining wisdom. Just as the bee does not waste time looking for pollen in a dead flower, the wise practitioner does not waste time just sitting with a blank mind. Just as the bee is untiring in its efforts, the serious practitioner works until he tastes the honey of wisdom. When the poet has brought his practice to fruition, he is transmitting and honoring the tradition of his sect. But fundamentally, what is he transmitting, and whom is he honoring? He is really transmitting the method discovered by the Buddhas, and he is honoring the Buddha nature that is intrinsic in all sentient beings.

This practice is called Silent Illumination.
It penetrates from the deepest to the highest.

These lines speak of faith — faith in a tradition of practice that has been handed down without interruption from the Buddha on through countless generations. Is there anyone who can practice it and not find in it all of the Buddha Dharma, from the deepest to the highest?

PART
THREE

Retreat Reports

D.S.

I approached the Ch'an retreat with a mixture of excitement and apprehension. I was excited at the prospect of what a week of meditation could do for me; but I was wary of the kind of commitment or loss that I might have to face. This commitment, I knew, could be capable of evoking the most profound sort of agony and insecurity. Generally no person is completely willing to cast everything away, to stand alone and search for himself anew. We always try to hold something back, whether it be in the form of a hope, fear, guilt, complacency, love, or hate. Like some great Rock of Gibraltar, it's our last refuge before the unknown of open sea.

On the first day my suspicions were confirmed. The Master presented a new face to us — stern, dignified, and sharpened with the greatest urgency. No longer was he so patient and tolerant; rather the ultimatum was simple and direct:

> In this week you can become enlightened
> if you wish. There is no doubt about this.
> You must forget everything else, and

> without concern for body or mind, throw
> your whole self into this question. If you
> do anything less than make a total effort,
> then you will waste this most precious
> opportunity. If that is the case, then you
> should not be here!

I was surprised and frightened at what he had done.
The Master had stolen our complacency, and thrown
this one essential decision entirely upon us. In view
of the respect that I have for the Master, myself, and
our relationship, how could I possibly shirk this
responsibility?

For a number of years Buddhist studies has been
my life's work. I felt in the past that I had some
understanding of the matter of man's spiritual life,
and could make some contribution to its study. But
how could I ever really dare to conjecture about and
teach Buddhism, or speak about practicing Buddhism, if I couldn't even summon the integrity and
courage to face the single most essential issue? I
would be the greatest liar to even think to discuss it.

Such thoughts as these began to boil up in my
mind. The week passed in a turmoil of emotions.
Sometimes I felt guilty or condemned, incurably
corrupt and weak. Sometimes I was very sad, or
angry and frustrated. Sometimes I felt regretful, and
sometimes I felt exalted and full of bliss.

Sometimes I felt as if I had gone too far. There
was no possibility of finding comfort in turning back.

All security was gone, and I looked on, terrified, as if some abyss of incurable insanity yawned before me. Everything was different, and I felt very shaken and in awe of the true immensity of the question we were asking. It was no toy, but very serious indeed! Could I really trust these strange bald-headed people speaking a different language, and with mannerisms different from anything I had known? What if the Master misunderstood, or wasn't really in control!

Daily I poured these emotions out to the Master; I never felt so emotionally raw and exposed. Sometimes he would console me, sometimes praise me, and sometimes confront me in the most direct and devastating manner. Often I was terrified of the interview.

One evening my meditation got very powerful. I felt a huge flow of energy and bliss, and I was very taken in by it all. I was sure I would make it in the very next meditation period. I sat anxiously through the Master's evening lecture – it went on and on. Even when we entered the meditation hall he kept talking. When was he going to stop and let us sit! As the time approached, the energy and assuredness grew. I sat down as if I was never coming back again, certainly I would have a great enlightenment! I concentrated with all my might; the energy welled up and I could feel it pounding at the top of my skull. I pushed harder and harder, and didn't dare to let go, just waiting and struggling for what must come! Suddenly I just gave out and collapsed, exhausted. The pain was extraordinary. "What a fool," I thought, "What a self-righteous overblown fool. You are filled with demons and corruption." That night I went to sleep.

The next morning the Master asked me what had happened the previous night, and how late I stayed up meditating. I told him, and he showed absolutely no sympathy. He looked straight at me, right into me, and said, "I told you that sleep was not a concern for you. Who told you to sleep? In China some people forego sleep for ninety days, and you can't do it for even part of a week. Here you get a little experience in meditation (imitating me). Oh, I sit Ch'an! and give up, thinking you've got something. It's nothing! You simply have no determination for the Path!"

The last words hit me like a bolt of lightning. I was devastated, so ashamed. There it was, right out in the open, all the doubt, fear, and weakness that I so skillfully hid from myself and others. The issue was actually very clear and straightforward – Do I really want liberation? I could feel all the old obstructions pulling at me: love of women, fear of family pressure, love of leisure, attachment to friends, fear for my life, etc. Yet, truly, liberation was most important. I made up my mind; there was no further need for emotional dramatics and display. The question of enlightenment became intensely personal, more so than it had ever been before. I felt this desire for freedom and liberation from deep down inside.

The next day, around mid-morning, I was sitting

in meditation, somewhat sleepy, when suddenly I woke up and a cool calm came over me. "If I really want liberation, then this searching for some grand 'Wu' is totally absurd. All this Buddhism, this picturesque myth, has to go. All these years I've enslaved myself. I cannot sit here any longer. I must talk to the Master." I felt shaken up, but resolved and fresh. I wanted to roar at my foolishness — the whole world I had so carefully constructed and maintained about myself. The Master walked into the room; I pointed at him and said I wanted to speak to him. We went into the interview room. I was exploding, birds were singing outside. I sat opposite him, full front, and said, "Buddhism really is empty isn't it?" He broke into a smile, I was just bubbling forth to him. I wanted to grab him by the shoulders and shake him, embrace him; there was so much pouring out. He said, "Congratulations, you finally have something, a very, very small bit of fruit." I said, "But I still have doubts!" He said, "Forget them, don't worry. You may go outside and wander around. Don't sit any-more."

I was shaken; I felt wild like a raging beast. I said, "I'm going!" and stormed through the hall and out the door. I wandered aimlessly. The sky was over-cast, the day chilly and windy. A lone crow cawed wildly at me from a tree-top. The whole world was in raw untameable motion. I felt completely exposed and alone. I went to the cliff overlooking the ocean. The wind howled fiercely through the trees, and waves rushed across the bay. I felt what it was like to be homeless.

I slept, and that evening the sky had cleared and all was calm. At dusk D.W. and I walked to the cliff. We found a large boulder and sat looking across the bay, out to sea, speechless. The evening was gentle, and everything so fresh and at peace. The air was rich with the smell of the ocean and the sky alive with the cool shades of dusk. It was all so clear. Finally we started back down the beach. I could feel the small stones beneath my feet, worn round and smooth by the waves. I picked one up; it had a slight dimple on one side. It seemed such a perfect expression of the way I felt, of everything. I thought to take it with me, held it tightly in my hand, and started up the hill. But it really bothered me. I knew I just couldn't keep it. It was wrong. Halfway up the cliff I threw the rock way out, watched it arc through the dusk, and heard it clatter on the beach below, where it belonged. I felt good.

R.A.

I first heard about meditation retreats from friends whose accounts were varied, and some spoke about unpleasant experiences. Not wanting to be influenced by these stories, I came to Master Sheng-yen's retreat with no expectations. Whatever happens, I would do my best and get whatever I could from the experience.

When we arrived at Bodhi House, I was overwhelmed by its beauty. But on seeing the schedule, I didn't know if I could get up at four A.M. and sit ten hours a day. To my surprise, as the days went on I sensed a spiritual energy growing. I wouldn't say it was the house itself, but it occurred to me that this was a place where people came to get enlightened! The schedule was all right for me. I slept well, woke up with enough energy to get through the day's work. I say "work" because that's what it was, since we practiced almost constantly.

On the second day while concentrating on the breath, I started feeling numb, as though I was a corpse wrapped in cotton, except I could still see. I thought of how it feels to be dead. I thought of my father and how he felt when he died. Tears started to come. I didn't move. Master Sheng-yen motioned me into the interview room. When I told him what happened, he said that's in the past, concentrate on the present. Though I knew that already, the sternness he maintained in the zendo changed to such compassion that I felt greatly relieved and went back to sit.

The schedule became a steady flow of activities. At bedtime we practiced lying down until we fell asleep, only to wake up a few hours later to the sound of wooden boards being clapped. I began to feel a lightness of body. I lost my appetite, but I ate a little anyway to maintain the daily routine. Once, when Master Sheng-yen took us outside for slow walking meditation, I felt like an infant taking its first wonderful steps. I saw trees, pebbles, grass, colors, so clearly, as though for the first time. Everything seemed fresh and new.

Sometimes in the afternoon, I would wonder if I could sit any longer. Once, in intense pain, I said to myself, "I'll sit here until my legs fall off, then I won't be bothered by them!" It helped; the pain gradually lessened. Another time, Master Sheng-yen told us not to worry if we died, that he would take all the responsibility. "Well," I thought, "if he's going to be responsible, I'll sit here till I die." It may seem ridiculous, but it helped my sitting. I sat with a lot of determination after that.

In our first interview, Master Sheng-yen asked me why I came. I said the first thing that came to me: "To improve my practice." He said, "I hope you will have higher goals." I left feeling foolish. During our free period after lunch, I thought about why I came. Then it occurred to me that this place, this schedule, this teacher, were all positive conditions for enlightenment! It was all up to us! The next day, Master Sheng-yen again asked me why I came. "Hopefully to get enlightened," I said. "Yes. Now work hard," was all he said.

In the zendo I felt the oneness of everyone, like one person sitting instead of ten. Then Master Sheng-yen would hit me on the shoulder with his stick and that thought would be zapped out of my head. He once told us we were all stupid. He said we outnumbered Reverend Jih-Ch'ang and himself and could easily beat them up with their sticks. Instead we all sat and got hit by them.

After dinner one evening, instead of walking to the ocean, as I sometimes did, I sat on the grass and meditated. I vowed that I wouldn't move until I got enlightened. I sat and watched the grass become individual blades of grass, to a mass blur of green, to a bright light. I felt I was the Buddha. I was conscious of a total space in front of me, surrounding me, in me, and then I felt there was no space. One single tear slid from my eye, down my cheek, landing on my leg. I kept sitting, but I could focus only on what was in front of me. Soon Reverend Jih-Ch'ang was ringing the bell for the lecture to begin.

Master Sheng-yen reminded us that our time was limited, how our good causes and conditions gave us this chance. He warned us that if we didn't seize the opportunity it may never come again. I was concerned about my ability to function well the next day if I stayed up all night. Master Sheng-yen stressed that there was no health danger in sitting all night. After that I sat a little longer each night before going to sleep.

Near the end of retreat, I stayed up sitting for a long time. I was using all my energy concentrating on *Wu*, and had no other thoughts. Still, I was angry at myself and felt I should be working harder. I finally started nodding out, and went upstairs to sleep. But before I knew it, the boards were clapping and it was time to get up again. I didn't feel tired. I didn't feel very energetic either. At breakfast, my nose began to bleed. I got up and washed, then sat down at the table.

During the interview Master Sheng-yen told me to go outside for a rest, but I didn't want to stop sitting because of a stupid nose-bleed! I figured, well, I'll never get anything now. He interrupted my thoughts and told me to relax and not think of anything. I had planned to stay up all night, but Master Sheng-yen said there was still time; I should go to sleep and work hard the next day.

Outside, I looked at the flowers on the dogwood trees. Some were buds shut tightly, others were just blossoming, while some were fully bloomed. I thought of how we were like those flowers, trying to cultivate our own true nature. They bloom naturally, revealing their nature. Though following a strict schedule, we were living a very natural life, using each day entirely, not wasting a moment. When we sat ready to eat the food we'd prepared, I usually felt I had earned the meal by working hard.

Near the end of the retreat, Master Sheng-yen told us that he and Reverend Jih-Ch'ang were shepherds trying to get their sheep up a tree, because there was no more grass to eat. He was in the tree pulling and Reverend Jih-Ch'ang was at the bottom pushing. He said, "Come on up, the leaves taste sweet! But you sheep say, 'Ah, I'm too tired.'" He told us he couldn't pull anymore. We were on our own. It's all up to us! I was determined to try.

When I went back to sit I shut out everything except "What is *Wu*? What is *Wu*? What is *Wu*?" It started changing and I lost the words: "What is blue? One and two." suddenly, it didn't matter. Nothing mattered. My eyes, ears, nose mouth all blended to one. I felt like a deflated balloon. I started shaking and began to cry. Reverend Jih-Ch'ang hit me. Harder than he did all the other times. I was crying effortlessly. I was told to follow Master Sheng-yen. Once inside the interview room I started to laugh. Master Sheng-yen and Reverend Jih-Ch'ang smiled at me. Revered Jih-Ch'ang smacked me on the shoulder the way a parent would show they are pleased with their child's efforts. I bowed to Master Sheng-yen. I was close to his feet and wanted to hold them in my hands and kiss them. I wanted to hug them both.

At lunch, I ate but it didn't seem like food. After the meal, Master Sheng-yen told me to go into the zendo because my work wasn't finished. I didn't know what to think or feel. Just what is *Wu*? So once again, I sat. I wasn't sitting long, when master Sheng-Yen took me into the interview room. He said that I should relax, take a bath and come back at three o'clock. I went to the woods where I could see the ocean and the beach below. It was more beautiful than ever. I met Dan. We talked about Buddhism and animals we'd seen that day. I don't think either of us was making too much sense, but it didn't matter!

When the retreat was over, I felt very close to everyone. I think that closeness was also felt by everyone else. Master Sheng-yen described it as a dream we all shared. Now the dream is over. It is.

K.S.

On the drive to Bodhi House I felt a strange lack of excitement even though I had looked forward to this opportunity for a long time. Perhaps now I was frightened of being transformed, of having to abandon my desires. Anyway I resolved to work hard on the strength of my desire for enlightenment. At first the daily routine seemed ominous; I was afraid I would not remember all the instructions, or complete my chores. But after a day I became acclimated, and was grateful there was no time for daydreaming. We were not allowed to talk, but this suited me since conversation sometimes created barriers, rather than real communication, between people. Paradoxically, in silence, there seemed to be a greater sense of community, and responsiveness to people's needs.

After a few days I was no longer distracted by thoughts of my outside life. During this time I was practicing the method of watching my *tan-t'ien*. I became very centered and calm, but I had a slight nervousness before my interviews with Shih-fu, which was dispelled as soon as we were face to face. I would tell him that I was not getting anywhere with my meditation. I was worried that I would not achieve any results. He would tell me not to worry about the future, just concentrate on the method. My concentration was improving, but I was impatient because the schedule was too predictable, and Shih-fu seemed too easy with me. There did not seem to be any room for the unexpected. For instance, I would relate some experience I had, while sitting or in a dream, since I had last spoken to him. But whatever I related was already in the past. When would the immediate experience, the real interaction take place?

One day during slow walking, I became aware of everyone else's *tan-t'ien*. I suddenly felt that everything was flimsy and transparent. I felt there was something wrong with what everyone was doing, that they had to go through so much suffering on the retreat. At lunch, I thought it was ridiculous how everyone was enjoying their food. Shih-fu said that these feelings showed that some deep-seated jealousy had come to the surface. This explanation surprised me, but then I realized that jealousy had always been an obstacle of mine. Part of my worries stemmed from my fear that Shih-fu did not want me to get enlightened at all – that he was being too nice. Maybe he had different plans for the people that he disciplined more strongly. Of course, I was very ashamed of these feelings.

What saved me was the strongest thing I had going for me – my faith in Shih-fu. My meditation was always best just after the interview or the evening lecture. Perhaps because of previous karmic connections, I had very early developed a strong attachment to Shih-fu. When Shih-fu left for Taiwan only six weeks after I met him, I was very upset and had many fears that something would prevent his return. But eventually my happiness at finding a teacher after a lifetime of doubt began to override my fears. I was convinced that he was my Shih-fu, that I would never seek another one. If he did not return, I would accept it. Maybe I was not destined to become enlightened in this lifetime. In this way, faith came to my rescue once before.

It seemed that now I was beginning to lose faith because of my selfishness. One evening, Shih-fu called me into the interview room. He indicated by his questions that he knew that I was sitting well just then. I was awed by his perception, and this brought me out of my fears that Shih-fu was not being attentive to me. I decided to trust him entirely. I recalled from one of the evening lectures his image of some people who impatiently grasp for enlightenment as if it were some glorious fruit. It dawned on me that I was impatient for the same reason – I selfishly desired the fruit of enlightenment. Even if I got the fruit, what use would it be? There is no point getting enlightened unless it can benefit all sentient beings. The least I could do was to be a little patient.

The next day Shih-fu gave me the kung-an "What is *Wu*?" As soon as I used it, my perception of meditation changed. Previously, I only felt that I was seriously meditating when I was sitting. Now the method was constantly with me. There was no transition between sitting or doing chores. They were just arbitrary things I was doing with my body. Still, I worried that I was not asking the question correctly, or with enough conviction. That afternoon, while I was sitting, Shih-fu spoke in Chinese to someone behind me. I heard the word *kai-wu* (enlightenment) and I suddenly thought: This retreat is the real thing! If I don't exert all of my strength now, there will never be another time!

I started asking with a vengeance: "*Wu, wu,* what is *wu? Wu, wu,* what is *wu?*" I followed Shih-fu's instructions to ask the question as if I were pumping air into a tire; if there was no more room left, I should pump more air in. My body became very tense and sweaty and I rocked in my seat. When I thought I could not go on, I forced myself to ask it again. Suddenly Shih-fu hit me with his incense board twice on each shoulder. I did not experience any pain, just the sound of a loud, hollow crack, completely stopping all my thoughts.

I looked up at Shih-fu. He told me to stand up. I followed him to the interview room, where I promptly sat down. Shih-fu waved the stick in front of me. "What am I holding?" I stared at it blankly. It is hard to describe what I felt. I knew what it was, my being tangibly felt exactly what it was, but there was no word that I could find for it. I tried to say something, my mouth opened and closed, but nothing came out. Finally I just laughed and waved my arms in surrender. The same thing happened when he asked me what I was sitting on. he asked me if I was happy, and I shook my head, "No." It seemed that nothing had really happened. He said I was very quick, but not strong enough yet. I went back to the meditation room.

After this, I did not feel changed in substance, but my priorities changed so radically, they almost went in reverse. I felt I could no longer make my worldly desires the primary consideration, but should dedicate my life to following the Dharma. Pain and sleepiness no longer hindered my meditation. I developed a disregard for my body. I felt that it was no longer my own since I had dedicated it to the service of all other beings.

Now I understood that compassion was not an extra thing that one should cultivate besides meditation; it was indispensable to the success of the meditation itself. It could not work or have any significance without it. At supper the food had no flavor; its texture was almost like water. Shih-fu had reminded us that day that the evening meal was called "medicine." It came to me that Shih-fu and Jih-Ch'ang Fa-shih were doctors and Bodhi House was like a sanatorium where we were all recuperating from an illness that we had never been aware of. Sometimes during our daily walk outside I was struck with a poignant sadness. The anguish and self-deprivation of the retreat, caused by our misery, made the grounds seem almost painfully beautiful in contrast. All the more so since we were not participating fully in the bliss of all the living creatures there — the caterpillars, butterflies, trees, hares, and especially the surprising multitude of birds whose unusual calls comforted me during the day.

The next day I was more relaxed and joy was replacing sadness. Just doing ordinary things made me so happy. I remember I was in the kitchen slicing carrots. I became aware that Shih-fu was standing there watching me. I experienced an unspoken flow of warm affection between us. Then I helped him boil some water for tea. I felt so buoyantly happy that we could share these simple things together. I feel that all the people on the retreat became very close, like a family. When the retreat was over I could not believe it. It had been only a week long, but it seemed as if I had lived a whole lifetime in another realm not located in ordinary time and space. Now it was time to test my new life in the outside world.

D.W.

A few years ago a friend and I were listening to music, enjoying a spontaneous, energized conversation. We were tripping, having ingested a type of LSD known as windowpane, in a dose that would last twelve hours. Suddenly my friend turned off the lights, because the overhead light was much too bright. I did not enjoy the darkened room, so I went into my own room to bring back a candle.

The moment I stepped into my own room my mind went "crazy": nothing had a name. The candle was still there and I went about my business, but I wasn't there – there was no Dan Wota. This unnerved me so much that after lighting the candle and taking it into the other room, I left and asked another friend, who was downstairs, to take a walk with me. I thought I was going crazy, that I was having a bad trip. I replayed the thoughts in my mind. They seemed illogical, and I concluded that I must be going insane. The walk helped tremendously, but the drug's effects were still going to last many hours. I felt paranoid, but all I could do was ride the trip out to the end.

Even after the drug was out of my body, the thoughts that there were no names and no Dan Wota were with me constantly. Actually, it wasn't that so much as my belief that I had gone crazy. For a year or so my mental condition was colored with intense fear and paranoia.

At this time I was aware of Buddhism and Ch'an, and had read much on both subjects. However, it would be over a year before meeting Shih-fu, and becoming his student. That interim was marked with an unusually painful inward struggle.

Previously, whenever I remembered the above episode I would cringe. It was one of the worst experiences of my life, with deep repercussions. Now I think of it as a blessing in disguise: it forced me to abandon my lifestyle, my involvement with drugs and alcohol, and edged me into pursuing the Dharma.

After being a student of Shih-fu's for a while, I attended my first retreat. On that retreat three people got very good results. I, on the other hand, came away with a great deal of disappointment. Not until later did I see that I also got a great deal of benefit. What stands out in my mind from that retreat is Shih-fu telling me, in one of the daily interviews, that I was working hard, but that I had an obstruction. He said that in the past, a Ch'an master would send someone like me away for five years to do hard labor. Fortunately, only a year later, I was able to attend a second retreat.

On the first morning I awoke to a familiar sound: two wooden boards being banged together. My first coherent thoughts were, "Here we go again," and "Why am I here?" One bit of conversation echoed from the night before. In presenting the use of the incense board to the newer students, Shih-fu had mentioned that another student and I were the type who needed to be hit often. Recalling the last retreat, I decided if constantly being hit was the shape of things to come, I had better work hard.

One of my regrets from the last retreat was that I hadn't worked hard enough, hadn't really pushed myself. This time, I told myself, it would be different. I would try to meditate past the ten o'clock bedtime. Even so, I didn't succeed in staying up all night; most nights I slept two or three hours.

Despite my efforts, most of the retreat I felt I wasn't working hard enough. Stray thoughts assailed me no matter what I was doing – sitting, walking, chanting, preparing a meal, or eating. However, throughout the retreat, Shih-fu consoled me and encouraged my efforts. At times I felt that he was just humoring me; that if he really wanted to help me he should be scolding me, instructing me to work harder. But he just asked about my health, and how I was coming along with my method.

Around the third day, I complained that I wasn't working hard enough, that I couldn't get myself to work harder, that I had stray thoughts of the past, plus the usual pain in my legs and back. Questions kept popping up like "Why am I here? What is all this for? Why am I going after some mysterious something I'm not supposed to think about? Am I doing the method correctly? Will I be a failure if I don't get something?" and on and on . . . . Shih-fu asked, "Do you feel stronger than the last retreat?" I realized I did, that I was no longer the same person who had come to the retreat three days ago. If anything was the turning point that was it. It gave me an added strength and self-confidence in the abilities I possessed, abilities which could definitely be used.

As I read back over what I've just written I think, "What a bunch of ego-inflated crap to lead the reader into believing that I was so fully aware of the situation, as if there was a blueprint I was able to follow." No such luck! Morning boards were sounded, I awoke and went about doing what had to be done just because it had to be done. I meditated — stray thoughts arose. I utilized my method and eventually less and less thoughts bubbled up. But there were certain themes to which I attached varying degrees of importance. (All very mundane stuff!) And in no manner was I able to view my efforts objectively. This is the importance of the master: to guide the student, to say what the student needs to hear and help him, whether it be scolding, kindness, or just leaving him alone.

A master is like a music teacher who sounds a particular musical chord which the student must attempt to perform. Without the master, a student might aimlessly search for the correct combination of notes, but just one clue from the master, "Put this finger here, this one here," and student and master strike the same chord in harmony. So the gratitude that I feel towards Shih-fu and the Three Jewels is inexpressible. Without Shih-fu's guidance I would still be clutching at ideas and things, seeking answers, rather than practicing and letting the harvest come naturally.

The fifth night, at the start of the lecture, Shih-fu said that the Karen we saw before us was not the same Karen as last night. A spasm of thoughts disturbed me: some form of disappointment, resentment, despair, past and future thoughts all rolled into one mass. Then another wave of thoughts: OK, she's answered Shih-fu's question to his satisfaction, I can too if I work hard enough. I just continued focusing my attention on the method. Both sides of the issue and all ensuing emotions were very real, begging me to acknowledge and attach to them. It would have been very comfortable to feel sorry for myself, but I knew that was a dead-end.

At the end of the lecture, Shih-fu talked about names. Turning to me he said, "What is your name?" After I was unable to answer, he waved his hands in an up-and-down motion about his body saying, "No name, just this . . . just this!" pointing to himself. This ended the lecture. In five minutes it would be time to sit again. I went to the bathroom, concentrating on my method. I thought, "No name, just this." I looked in the mirror and there was no Dan Wota. I walked downstairs to sit in meditation. Passing through the kitchen I saw that everything was still there, it hadn't disappeared, but it no longer presented a problem.

I sat for a while, and when I thought I was ready I stood up and asked Shih-fu to go to the interview room. After prostrations I presented my realization. Shih-fu offered, "Congratulations." And I replied, "Congratulations for nothing." We laughed.

On the beach, I stood on a boulder, looked at the World As-It-Is, without names, laughing. All I could say aloud was, "Thank God there is no Dan Wota!"

M.I.C.

I began the retreat in an exploring mood. I do not consider myself as serious a practitioner as my wife. But somehow I felt a little bit jealous when she talked about her retreat experiences. Seven days of four hours sleep, six meditation periods a day, no outside contact or talking, must be an adventure for anyone. If she could last through it with her poor health, why can't I? Sitting uninterrupted for forty minutes seemed to be an impossible task for me. I adjusted the mattress, the position of the cushion, and my poor legs, hoping to find a torture-free combination. There is no doubt, I can positively claim to be the most frequently moving object in the meditation hall. Shih-fu asked me to calm myself by concentrating on counting the breath. I started to apply the method to my breathing, but my mind did not begin to settle down until after supper.

After the evening lecture about five minutes into the evening meditation, a certain sensation of warmth diffused from the abdomen towards the upper body. I felt the acceleration of heartbeat, the blood vessels around the knee area flowing in pace, and, most important, all pain vanished without a trace. As a cat sunbathing in winter, I would not think to move my body even a tiny bit. My body and mind felt so great. I began to consider that the half-lotus might be one of the most natural postures to assume. "Is this the experience of Ch'an?" I kept on asking myself. If it was, then I must use the most advanced method, the kung-an "Wu," to investigate. I must be close to the door of Ch'an, otherwise such high and jubilant emotions would not arise at all. I remembered Shih-fu's Intermediate Class lecture on kung-ans. I cried out "Wu" soundlessly with all my heart. To my surprise, nothing happened. In deep frustration, I incorporated a nasal sound of "Wu" to each exhalation. The sound of "Wu" did not lead me anywhere, but definitely attracted the blows of Shih-fu's incense board on my shoulder.

An incomplete experience is worse than no experience at all. I spent most of the second day thinking of my previous experience and trying in vain to retrace the steps. Could I have lost the way to Ch'an completely? The only sensation that reminded me of the excitement was the piercing pain in my knees. I told myself that even if I did not recover the state of mind I had yesterday, I definitely had conquered the fear of pain once and for all.

When I was idling around the tea stand the next morning during the rest period, I noticed a framed Heart Sutra with seal-block print on the wall. I squeezed behind the teapot trying to identify all the

Chinese characters. The phrase *"hsin wu kua ai,"* no discrimination and no burden of mind, caught my sight. I said to myself "If there is no discrimination and no burden, what else could exist in the mind? Nothing! Nothing! Nothing!" I pondered on this sentence for about fifteen minutes before the meditation period. As sitting progressed, I used no method except the sentence and searched for an answer. My breathing gradually became refined. I felt cool and comfortable as each inhalation became a sting of icy water. That coolness settled down my body much more, but the sense of doubt of having nothing in the mind grew stronger. There must be something wrong. I felt a warmth before, and now the cooling sensation may guide me in the wrong direction.

I must have shown great doubt on my face when I was interviewed by Shih-fu. The first thing he said was: "What's happened?" I told him about the sentence and the cooling experience. I asked him what could exist in the mind besides discrimination and burden. He replied indirectly by saying that there must be something else in my mind and probably I had the wrong keywords. The correct one should be: "What is Wu?" I continued sitting with even greater doubt. I worked on, and was bored by the kung-an, but nothing happened. My thought was stuck on the sentence from the Heart Sutra.

Suddenly, a tremendous sense of emptiness overcame my mind. I suddenly felt that my heart was lost. That was the same kind of feeling I experienced when I lost my best friend in high school to pneumonia. That emotion was much deeper than sadness. I decided to quit thinking but I could not help it. I was desperate. I must consult with Shih-fu again. I asked him impatiently, "What have you done with me?" followed by, "Where is my heart?" Since Shih-fu was the only person to whom I had talked in the past few days, he must know where my heart was. He sensed my irritation and urgency and tried to persuade me logically be explaining the two types of heart loss – pure physical sensation or a temporary mental condition. "Work on *Wu*" was his final advice to me.

Next morning we did walking meditation outside. Meditation in a jungle of flying caterpillars must be one of the most absurd things under the sun. But that morning I was in a different mood. I wanted to walk as slowly as possible. Since I lost my heart in the meditation hall, I must look for it outdoors. I looked intently in front of my feet. Bypassing green caterpillars, ants, leaves and tree branches on the path, a single white-edged black crow feather jumped into my sight. I said to myself that since my heart without feet could not crawl out of my body, it must have flown out somehow. This feather might be what I was searching for. I had a sort of secret pleasure when I picked the feather up. I held it gingerly in my palm and examined it very closely. I started firing these questions to my mind: "Why do you think this feather is your heart – because of no sensation of crawling? Why didn't you pick up a caterpillar instead of a feather? Why?" I began to realize how discriminative I was.

Actually, everything is a reflection of my mind. My heart could be anything which I desired. Only an opened mind could lead to the state of no burden and no discrimination. When Shih-fu was gathering the answers to the question "Who is walking?" he got only one word from me, "Shih-fu." I was really mad at him at that time. My answer to the second question, "Where are we going?" was, "To my mind."

At lunch, I tried to follow Shih-fu's advice to eat each dish as if tasting it for the first time. To my surprise, I did it effortlessly, as I kept telling myself that my heart was everywhere, everything is a disposition of my mind. That was the most hearty meal of my life.

After lunch when I was wandering around between the dining room and the meditation hall, I saw some people standing or sitting there aimlessly just like me. Oh, my God. There was a genial warmth rising from the bottom of my heart. Those people were born, grown, and educated the same way as I was. Why could I not share my heart with them? Why do I treat them coldly like this? The tears started to fill my eyes as the feeling grew. I had to face the wall then, because I was overwhelmed by guilt.

In the interview room, when I described my feelings, I could not control myself, and burst into tears. Shih-fu asked me to prostrate. I did it in an awkward way and kept on crying loudly. I asked myself where the guilty feeling came from, and why I had to cry. I had no answers.

I wanted to show him that feather so eagerly but I could not find it in my pocket anymore. Oh! I lost my heart again! No! My heart can be anything and it can reach anywhere. There was no need to carry that piece of feather anymore. Shih-fu smiled in such an understanding way that any explanation was unnecessary. He taught me that the emotion which I experienced was generated out of compassion. I should always guard and cherish it. I have never felt so grateful to anybody as I did to Shih-fu. He asked me to relax and take a walk outside. I followed his instructions.

When my emotion began to calm down, I noticed the world became so beautiful and friendly. The sky, the wind, the oak trees, and the grass all greeted me with smiles as if they were saying, "Welcome home, brother." I was fortunate to see, to hear, to taste, to smell, and to touch them. I recognized them because we all came from the same origin. Standing under a pine tree, I lost the feeling of disgust for the caterpillars. I swore not to condemn the yelling crows again. I accepted them without reservation.

I joined the slow walking line with a smile. I felt so grateful to my fellow practitioners, yet I had so little to offer them. I cherished every moment to be with them.

While we were resting on the lawn, Shih-fu asked who could see the sun through the clouds. I looked very hard at the direction of the sun. I could not see it, but I sensed that ever-radiating warmth.

I continued to think about the unselfish sun in the meditation period. Then I felt both my body and mind start to drift away. What a weird kind of feeling it was! I wanted to say something, but I could not. The next thing I remembered was that I was riding along with a bright comet across the galaxy. The brightness, beyond description, shone through space and left no dark spot or shade in the universe. I could see the back of a leaf and internal organs of the caterpillar with ease. I scanned through the valley of death and the words of Jesus came to my mind. I have seen the darkest corner of the valley. I had no fear of death at all.

I wanted to find where I was. I saw the stream of time-space continuum across the cosmos without beginning and end. I realized the true meaning of causation and the concept of karma. There were no conflicts or dilemmas to resolve. There were numerous folds of universes, with unique dimensions of infinite time and infinite space, in coexistence. Each set of the universe could be classified as either a sub-universe or co-universe simultaneously. They were not mutually exclusive, yet they could be distinctly and accurately defined as independent universes. All the characteristics found in one universe were transformable to another. Uniqueness transmuted into

wholeness and wholeness transmuted into uniqueness in ascending order forever. I recalled a poem by
William Blake:

> *To see a World in a grain of sand*
> *And Heaven in a wild flower*
> *Hold Infinity in the palm of your hand*
> *And Eternity in an hour.*

My tears flowed out naturally with compassion. One
moment was too long for eternity. I was reborn in
absolute freedom. I prostrate to all sentient beings.

M.H.

This had been my second retreat. Knowing how difficult things can get, I was motivated by fear as much as greed this time. I wanted to get as much pain as I could over with as soon as possible. Not very admirable, but it seemed to help. I think the energy I gathered the first few days almost carried me through the rest of the week. It's kind of beautiful when one's self-attachment (expressed as greed or fear) can be so instrumental in learning to become less self-attached.

I don't remember much about the beginning of the week (my retentive powers aren't that great — a real plus when participating on a retreat). I had been working on the kung-an "Where am I?" I think it was the fourth day during a meditation period when I suddenly felt I was on the verge of some kind of understanding, but I couldn't find any words for it. I let the feeling pass. Later that day I was in one of the kitchens cleaning the drinking glasses. Each person was assigned a specific glass solely for their use during the retreat. I picked up the first glass. My name was on it. I began to laugh. That's where

Marina was, in the sink! I had no name. It was as if the way I perceived things was becoming a little looser, freer.

That evening and the next day I began to feel strange during the meditation periods, although, at the time, I don't think I was aware of feeling strange. I'm not good at making analogies, but: Imagine someone has just skipped a flat rock across the surface of a pond. That rock is analogous to the mind. Each time the rock hits the surface of the water it believes it's a rock, it feels the water. When it's in the air it doesn't know anything. The words "rock," "air," and "water" cease to exist. It may be hard to see the value in having a mind that's like a flat rock in mid-air that doesn't know anything. But it's easy to understand that it's with words that we discriminate, draw boundaries, keep things frozen in time and space. As a result, we feel deprived and isolated.

While some of these mental habits seem to diminish, others come sharply into focus. Each day my selfishness stands out very clearly. I'm grateful for this because it's the only way I'll learn to unlearn it. I'm grateful for many things, but particularly grateful for the growth that is possible.

L.H.

On the first day of my second week-long meditation retreat with Master Sheng-yen, the intensity of the kung-an, the repeated questioning "Who-am-I" continued at the high level that had developed during the first retreat, one month before. Shih-fu helped to sustain and deepen this intensity by asking me to practice as a matter of life and death, reminding me that one never knows when or if such an opportunity will present itself again in this lifetime.

Many times the question "Who-am-I?" would burst into flames, and tears of spiritual commitment would spring from my eyes, almost turning to steam in the heat of my longing to get to the bottom of this primordial question which all beings are asking, consciously or unconsciously, and which even the universe itself is asking by its very existence. I did not feel caught up in an isolated personal quest but felt very near the center of the universal quest of human beings and, indeed, all conscious beings. But various spiritual experiences of peace and insight would arise and put out the flames of the kung-an, and I would suffer the illusion that these were answers to the question. Shih-fu relentlessly yet kindly attempted to turn my attention away from these spiritual experiences back to the sheer intensity of the practice "Who-am-I?"

These experiences were like wandering from the path to look at beautiful flowers or inspiring vistas. At this rate, one might never reach the end of the path. The master told me that if the flames of "Who-am-I?" die down, I must not simply accept this as part of the process but kindle them again with the torch of my own intense determination. The fire must become so vast that everything is consumed.

The talks Master Sheng-yen gives during retreat are particularly potent for everyone, and convey important personal messages to each practitioner. This does not occur through the ordinary thinking process but, as Shih-fu himself says, is like throwing a ball that one must actually catch with the entire body and mind without knowing what direction this ball is coming from. On the second or third evening of the retreat, Master Sheng-yen asked who had experienced sadness that day. I did not raise my hand because I had been experiencing simply the torrent of desperate longing for the Truth, interspersed with periods of peace and insight. But Shih-fu's message got through to the deeper layers of my being, because during the meditation period that followed the evening talk, I indeed experienced great sadness.

The problem I have of leaning slightly to the right during meditation began to concern me more deeply.

This problem comes from years of sitting in meditation alone, with no one to correct my physical posture. But it is more than that. It dramatizes the deepest level of personal illusion, because when I am leaning to the right, I feel confident that I am perfectly upright. This illusion persists not only with eyes closed but also with my eyes completely open. Suddenly, I felt deep sadness that I do not know who I really am, that the ideas and perceptions about which I was so sure were not true. As I continued to ask the question "Who-am-I?" I shed tears of sadness from the heart rather than tears of determination from the will. I was asking the question more deeply than ever before. When I reported this experience to Master Sheng-yen in his interview room, far from consoling me, he intensified my mood by stating clearly and convincingly that every thought and action since my very birth had been similarly off the mark – that I had lived my entire life in the realm of the false, imagining it to be true.

I accepted his statement and immediately felt a burden of intellectual and spiritual pride, that I was not even aware of carrying, fall away. With his subtle perception, Shih-fu saw that this purification had been accomplished, and he told me to forget the whole thing, that it was merely a mood, and I should simply return to the practice of "Who-am-I?"

Pushing forward more and more strongly with the kung-an, I often experienced the flames of determination raging for several hours on end. Finally, on the morning of the sixth day, with not only my whole mind but my whole body, with all its muscles and nerves, riveted on the question "Who-am-I?" there was a sudden release. The words clearly presented themselves: "There is nothing there." All tension dissolved as the phrase repeated itself: "There is nothing. There is nothing." There was a direct experience of what the Prajnaparamita Sutra teaches: there is really no body, no mind, no universe. I both laughed and wept as I experienced the radical nature of this resolution, or disappearance, of the question "Who-am-I?" A totally new realm presented itself, the realm of *prajnaparamita* or Perfect Wisdom. For several hours I sat in utterly quiet and balanced meditation, but there was no I, no body sitting in the zendo, no process of meditation, no universe. As the Heart Sutra expresses it: "No wisdom, no attainment, no path." I felt no need to report this to Shih-fu, because it was perfectly clear and self-authenticating, and there really was no Shih-fu and nothing to report.

Master Sheng-yen then asked all of us in turn, "Where is your mind?" I answered directly from the experience that nothing exists: "Nowhere!" Shih-fu asked me immediately: "Who says this?" Just as immediately, and with deep conviction, I answered: "Nobody!" Shih-fu again questioned: "What about the body that speaks these words?" The answer came: "There is no body!" The master turned aside and remarked: "Empty."

Just before this I had been doing fast walking (with no one walking and no zendo to walk in), when Shih-fu shouted "Stop!" Right before me was the scroll of Bodhidharma, and my eyes were gazing at the long fingernail on the third finger of his right hand. Shih-fu had then asked, "Where is your mind?" and I had answered inwardly, "In the third fingernail of Bodhidharma's right hand." When I told this to Master Sheng-yen later, he said that this was a correct answer to the question, not the other series of answers I had given. He told me to let go of the experience of emptiness and continue to question "Who-am-I?" with strong effort.

Later that afternoon, on the final full day of retreat, I was to be led further into the realm of Ch'an towards which Bodhidharma's fingernail had been pointing. The realm of Ch'an is completely different from the perfect stillness and emptiness of *prajnaparamita*, where one does not even experience peace, for there is no one to experience it. The realm of Ch'an is a realm of laughter. For several hours while seated in the meditation hall I was swept with wave after wave of laughter at the wonderful impossibility of everything. Given the Truth that nothing really exists, we are presented with an endlessly varied universe, whose existence is impossible yet whose appearance is vividly undeniable. The utterly quiet, primordial expanse of Emptiness is continually surprised as when a big stone is thrown into a still pond or colorful rockets explode in black space. Like a child, one can only laugh in sheer delight.

My brief foray into the realm of Ch'an was sparked by remembering a line from an ancient poem that Master Sheng-yen had given me three years before. For one year I had only the Chinese. The following year Shih-fu gave me the translation, which was something like this: "The bridge is flowing and the stream is standing still. Beneath the water, the moon is shining, and fish are leaping in the sky." It had been just a bizarre Zen poem to me then, but now, another year later, it became an igniting flame. I felt I might be going slightly crazy. I felt like a train that had left its tracks and was flying through the sky. I saw the world in the opposite way from the habitual view of the conventional mind. I was sure that stones floated up into the sky and feathers plunged to the bottom of the ocean. The oxen were eating rice with chopsticks and the farmers were grazing on grass. The children on the street were wielding the incense board and Shih-fu was throwing firecrackers in the zendo. I laughed and laughed and laughed, while the swift flow of "Who-am-I" continued in the background. At one point, two cars on the street had a humorous conversation with their horns. I started laughing again, but this time the other meditators in the zendo began laughing with me. My laughter wasn't just subjective. The world really is this funny.

The Zen teaching-story came to mind about the Master who killed a cat because none of his students could demonstrate the spirit of Ch'an in order to save it. Later, when his principal student returned from a journey, the master asked him how he would have saved the cat. The student placed his own grass sandals on his head and walked out. The master remarked: "If he had been here, the cat would have been saved." I saw clearly the spirit of this action. Our habitual way of viewing the world must be reversed. Sandles belong on the head, not on the feet.

The last night of retreat, I sat in meditation right through till the dawn, sitting, smoothly and deeply questioning "Who-am-I?" and refusing to allow myself to be diverted into spiritual experiences of any kind. No more tears, no more laughter. The next morning, I felt like a stick of incense burning in an empty room, like the sound of firecrackers in the streets, like a human being who eats and sleeps. What is there to realize? The retreat was over, so there was no opportunity for an interview. But I'm sure Master Sheng-yen would have said: "Return to the question, "Who-am-I?"

Bhiksu C.C.

September 1

Before the retreat, Shih-fu explained how we were to practice. During this talk, he revealed that by the end of this retreat, at least one person would enter the door of Ch'an. His tone was so firm I couldn't help thinking, "Has Shih-fu already seen what is going to happen? All right, let's wait and see." I started every sitting with a prostration and a vow: "Homage to the Buddhas, the Dharma, and the Sangha. Homage to Bodhisattva Ksitigarbharaja."

Tonight, right after sitting down, I felt I was sitting better than I did during my first retreat, three weeks ago. I had a firm grasp of the counting the breath method. The numbers came smoothly and continuously; there were wandering thoughts, but they couldn't interrupt my method. Suddenly, "Ding!" The bell cut through the silence of the meditation hall. My chest, especially the nerves around my heart, received the strong vibrations of the bell, and then I heard the sound. The two things happened simultaneously, but my mind clearly discerned them as separate events.

September 2

Counting the breath was smooth, continuous. Distinct wandering thoughts or "What is *Wu*?" occasionally interfered. I cautioned myself: "Just keep counting!" Thus alerted, I applied single-mindedness towards everything else — eating, walking, sweeping, everything. The experience with the bell did not recur as strongly, but my chest vibrated distinctly with each "ding!"

In the last sitting I totally forgot the environment. Eventually, I stopped counting. By then the coarser wandering thoughts were gone. Soon, I was unaware even of my body. Only fine wandering thoughts remained, and they became much clearer. After a few such experiences, I made further progress. All recognizable thoughts were gone. Only very minute thoughts, which I could not identify, continued. There was now only a very subtle feeling of the mind existing. This was a very sensitive state. When I heard the slightest sound, the sense of body returned, but I felt relaxed and comfortable in every pore.

September 3

In the morning I frequently lost the sense of body, while the state of having only very subtle thought-currents came back once, but clearer than before. Several times an expanse of red or white light, bright as neon lights, appeared before me. In this light I once had a side-view of Shih-fu sitting. Lacking sufficient samadhi power, I couldn't see very clearly, but I felt Shih-fu's energetic blessing.

On this same morning, while energetically counting the breath, I had a sudden impulse to cry. Then the line: "Offering my body and mind to innumerable worlds; this is showing gratitude towards the Buddha" – rushed into my mind. Deeply moved, I began to cry. During interview, Shih-fu asked me why I cried. I described my feeling at that moment. He said, "You're a monk. Of course you should offer your body and mind to innumerable worlds. But if you just feel that way and don't practice the vow, if you stay selfish and lazy, then you're not worthy of monkhood!" I thanked Shih-fu for his compassionate blessing.

September 4

In the morning Shih-fu told us to prostrate to the Buddhas. However, I continued to sit. While everybody else prostrated, Shih-fu spoke in a tone both encouraging and reprimanding, until tears began to flow. The noise of crying filled the hall. Hearing all that crying, I suddenly wanted to scold these people. I tried to check myself but finally I shouted, "What is there to cry about?" That must have scared them somewhat. Shih-fu hit me twice with his incense board saying, "Do you know everything?" I started laughing and then said, "How funny. What is the use of crying?" And then I calmed down.

Another incense stick passed by. Shih-fu told us to start walking meditation. I was still sitting, now with a slight numbness in my arms. All of a sudden my body slumped. Although my mind was very clear, I had no control over my body. I just fell backward onto the floor. Lin, the retreat helper, came over to help me, but once his hand touched my forehead, I acted like a child and started crying loudly. In fact, I was howling, with my arms flinging, my legs sometimes kicking. I was well aware of the situation but couldn't control myself; I just felt that to cry was very natural, very relieving. After a while I stopped crying. Only then did tears come. I tried to continue sitting but Shih-fu told me to go out to see if the world was different. Lin carried me to the couch in the lecture hall and let me rest there.

Shih-fu's words hooked firmly onto my heart. I strained my nearsighted eyes but couldn't see how the world was different. But since Shih-fu said there was a difference, there must be a difference. Then the so-called "doubt" rose in my mind. Although I was urgent to resolve my doubt, I was not anxious. The thought came to me — "When the causes and conditions are ripe, each will receive the appropriate retributions." I also knew that Shih-fu was using all kinds of methods to find the "person," and still hoped I could participate in this "examination."

After a while, Shih-fu came into the lecture hall and said, "Chi-Ch'eng!" I stared at him.

"Who is Chi-Ch'eng?"

Those words shot into my heart. I mumbled "Don't know. . . don't know." I looked intently at my body, at my hands, feeling them so intimate, yet so distant.

"Who was speaking to me just now?"

"Don't know, don't know." Still looking carefully at myself, feeling like a stranger to myself. Murmuring, making a few gestures, I laughed, "How incomprehensible!" Suddenly my body fell forward. Shih-fu said kindly, "Be careful!" I replied, "Doesn't matter." This body isn't mine. So what if it fell?

Urgently wanting to know, I asked, "Shih-fu, have you found the 'person'?" I knew I was still not the person Shih-fu was looking for. He asked me, "Is there such a thing as up and down?"

"No!"

"Is there such a thing as the sky or the earth?"

"Where?"

I raised my head, looked at Shih-fu, his shining, powerful eyes shooting right at me. Right away I felt his compassion. I leapt down from my seat, prostrating to Shih-fu, my eyes holding tears, saying from within my heart, "Shih-fu, you are too compassionate! You are too compassionate!" I was thus kneeling and crying.

Shih-fu said a thing or two and left. I got up and sat on the couch. Suddenly, I sprang to my feet, filled with dissatisfaction, knowing I still hadn't found it. I slammed my hand on the table. "I won't take this!

I won't accept this! Until now I haven't even found the shadow!" I calmed down a little bit and ran out of the lecture hall. On the way to the meditation hall, a clear, direct thought flashed through my mind:

"I am Chi-Ch'eng. Chi-Ch'eng is me." Absolute! Definite! I have found it!

Very quickly I walked in and went straight to Shih-fu. Slapping my chest with my right hand I said, "I am Chi-Ch'eng!"

With loving-kindness, Shih-fu said, "You have found it!" Deeply touched once more by his compassion, I prostrated to Shih-fu. Then, facing the Buddhas, I said, "Prostration to all fellow practitioners!" With palms joined, I stood facing the Buddha statues.

"Prostration to the Three Jewels in all directions!"
"Prostration to parents of all previous lives!"
"Prostration to all sentient beings!"

The other practitioners were influenced by this atmosphere; the sound of sobbing filled the Ch'an hall. Having calmed down, I walked towards Shih-fu. "Shih-fu, I have found it!" "Congratulations." We held each other's hands firmly. I felt very very close to Shih-fu — not just physical closeness, but closeness of the minds.

Shih-fu told me I could leave the Ch'an hall. A burst of compassion filled my heart. I must let the others know, to encourage and urge them to build up their faith and Bodhi mind. Kneeling facing the

Buddhas, I said:

"Fellow practitioners, you must learn well. This is an opportunity rare in a millenium!" — To realize how rare this opportunity was and to treasure it.

"Shih-fu is a Bodhisattva coming to this world through his compassionate vows!" — To have absolute faith in Shih-fu.

"Sentient beings suffer so! How great are our responsibilities!" — To stimulate and encourage Bodhi mind.

"Offering our bodies and minds to innumerable worlds; this is showing gratitude towards Buddha." This sentence, uttered from the heart, touched everybody.

I was in a state of ineffable fullness and happiness. The tension, restlessness and irritability that used to bother me disappeared, as did the striving and struggle to make breakthroughs. I felt a natural impulse to share this fullness and happiness with others.

In the afternoon we did walking meditation outdoors. Previously, I ignored the trees and grass. I didn't care where I was going. Now everything was lovable. Yes, the world was different, but it hadn't changed. The mountains, earth, flowers, trees remained the same. It was the state of the mind that had changed. Seeing the leaves that drifted onto the path, I looked upon them fondly, like old friends I hadn't seen in years. When I accidentally touched them, I apologized. My feet automatically stepped around the ants. Even the pillars of the temple seemed endearing. I now understood the phrase: "Everywhere, there is no mind; everywhere, mind is functioning."

A memorable day! Today I experienced the state and life of "having found!" I am deeply grateful to Shih-fu's for his compassionate guidance.

Homage to the Buddhas, the Dharma, and the Sangha, to all venerable sages and monks.

I offer my body and mind to innumerable worlds, expressing my gratitude to Buddha and to all sentient beings.

Wishing that sentient beings depart from suffering,
I will not seek my own happiness.

While one sentient being has not attained Buddhahood.
I will not enter Nirvana.

Homage to Bodhisattiva Ksitigarbharaja.

PART
FOUR

Radio Interview

Station WBAI Interview: The Practice of Retreat

Editor's note: The following transcript consists of a radio interview of Master Sheng-yen conducted by Mr. Lex Hixon on radio station WBAI in New York City on June 21, 1981. Appreciation is hereby expressed to Mr. Hixon and WBAI for permission to publish this transcript.

LH: I am curious about the hidden principles behind the process of retreat and about the way people develop their practice on retreat – how their minds settle down and actually become "simple." I want to begin by asking you – when a person first comes on retreat with a scattered mind, how can you tell when that mind is settled down enough to begin practicing the method?

Shih-fu: On the very first evening of the retreat I always instruct the participants: Take all your

affairs of the past and future and put them tempo-
rarily aside. When you leave, you can pick them up
again. But during the seven days of retreat, don't
bother with them at all. But it's not easy for someone
just starting out to suddenly drop all thoughts of past
and future. Therefore I start by giving students a
method to cause their attention to switch from the
past and future into the present. Although outside
thoughts may still come up, one should just ignore
them and concentrate on the method.

At the beginning of the retreat I say: "Relax, relax,
relax." Relax the body, the nerves, and the mind. If
any problems come up, just relax and don't bother
with them. If you feel any discomfort, relax. If you
can stay relaxed, whenever a stray thought arises it
will very naturally disperse. Eventually these
thoughts will diminish. Don't try to suppress
thoughts. If you do, your meditation will grow worse
and worse. The most important thing is to relax and
just concentrate on the present moment, that is, the
method you are working on. Even practicing like this,
the average person who is new to the retreat will not
be able to fully settle down until the third day or so.
Of course there are those who have a good practice
who can settle down right from the start.

LH: But Shih-fu, one of the things I noticed on
retreat with you is that you were actually firing me
up, rather than asking me to relax. I felt that after
the first couple of days, after I had relaxed a bit, you

were encouraging me to work very hard. So how can you explain that difference – relaxing and working very hard?

Shih-fu: After a person has already settled into the practice I will then give him a "tense" method. The person's body and mind basically should still be relaxed. Nevertheless, his work on the method should be strenuous. After a person's mind is calmed down you can make him put a lot of effort on keeping his mind moving in one direction, on a specific method. If you can single-mindedly go forward without slackening, then your power will get greater and greater and the results go deeper and deeper. When I see someone working like this, I might use all kinds of methods to goad him: shouting, scolding, anything to keep him from stopping or letting up. There is a Chinese saying: If your boat is going upstream, you better keep rowing, or you'll slip back with the current. It's like practice. You keep pushing forward. Otherwise your human inertia will just pull you right back.

LH: This is why a retreat master who is sensitive is so essential. During my retreat, after my mind and body had settled down enough for Shih-fu to get me into this more strenuous, single-minded practice, something happened. I lost the connection, and though I used my will power to stir up that strong practice again, it wouldn't happen. Shih-fu suggested that I relax again for a while. I thought I was going to lose the whole thing, but I relaxed again, and then, spontaneously, the more strenuous effort began to happen. So a retreat master knows just when to tell you to relax and when to goad you into strong effort, and they might alternate back and forth in a very complex manner.

From what I could see, it was masterful how Shih-fu worked very closely with the dozen or so people during the entire retreat, even seeming to know exactly when people went to bed and when they got up. Not through any occult power necessarily; he's just aware of everything that's going on. When the guidance is very fine, I think there can be nothing better than this kind of intensified practice.

After a strenuous period of sitting, Shih-fu instructs people how to massage themselves to regather their energy, and teaches them certain yoga techniques. Could you explain your connection with Chinese yoga?

Shih-fu: Certain kinds of exercises have always played an important part in many meditation traditions, such as T'ai Chi Ch'uan in Taoism, Shao Lin Temple boxing in the Ch'an sect of Buddhism, and yoga exercises in India. Also, for those who really develop good concentration, spontaneous movements will come naturally from their bodies from the meditation. Especially for beginners, it is a very good idea to coordinate exercise with meditation. It may not be necessary for someone who already sits very well. Beginners or inconsistent sitters may think they're relaxed, but are unconsciously tense, and the harder they work, the more tense they get. Also, because they are sitting immobile for a long time, problems may develop in various parts of the body, such as pain or poor circulation. Exercise is a good technique to correct these problems and keep the blood flowing throughout the body. The person whose concentration is very good will not have this problem − his blood will flow very smoothly.

LH: During the first few days I really got a lot from the exercises and it completely changed my attitude towards the body as an instrument for meditation. Usually when I meditate I tend to get away from the consciousness of the body, ignore it, but this really helped to integrate the body. Also the very fast and very slow walking in between sittings was a way of actually engaging the body in the meditative act. Maybe, Shih-fu, you could speak a little bit about fast and slow walking.

Shih-fu: In slow walking, a person's mind should sink downwards, figuratively speaking. When the mind sinks downwards, the spirit rises. Concentration moves downwards when we're doing the slow walking. Normally, people's minds are floating upwards, going out in all directions. This is a very scattered, flighty condition of mind, not at all stable. When the mind sinks downwards, it will settle down.

In fast walking, the body is very active, but the mind is still. I say, "Don't think. Just walk, the faster the better." The feet should be moving quickly, with very short steps. If you walk single-mindedly, thinking of nothing else, eventually you forget who is walking. At that time you may wonder, "Who is walking?" So this technique uses fast movement to get the person to forget himself, or at least forget his body.

LH: Seven days under these circumstances, being silent, eating sparingly, sleeping sparingly, the periods of quiet and intense sitting, the self-massage and yoga, the miles of fast walking, the combination of the whole thing, all began to have an incredible effect. Shih-fu told me earlier there are many details about the retreat that I don't know about — subtle details, that one would have to go on many retreats to be aware of. After all, I'm a complete neophyte, having only been on one of these retreats. So I'm just giving you the most obvious kind of report about it.

There are subtleties within subtleties as to how Shih-fu guides people. One example was the evening lecture, which had a peculiar quality of stimulating everyone's practice in an unusual way. So after a whole day of trying hard perhaps with little success, Shih-fu told us, and we felt this too, that usually our best sitting would come after hearing the talk. Shih-fu, could you explain what's going on in those talks and what you are doing for people on those talks?

Shih-fu: During the course of the retreat, there are many occasions when I say things to the group — while sitting, or privately. But the more important time is when I speak to everyone together in the evening. At that time I gather in everything that happened during the day, the various impressions I picked up, things that happened to people, and I say things indirectly to various people in the talk. I send messages, you could say, to the people sitting there. I rarely talk about Buddhist or Ch'an theory, and I don't talk about matters not concerned with the retreat. I concentrate on the things that people are experiencing, physically and mentally, and my talks are directed to these experiences.

However, I always start from a certain piece of literature, usually from Ch'an Buddhism, such as *Faith in Mind,* or the *Song of Enlightenment.* In theory the lecture is based on this, but I just use it as a springboard to talk about the things that are happening on the retreat. For instance, someone who is sitting there listening may feel very fatigued. I would say something, indirectly, that advises him how to overcome fatigue. If I see someone who feels discomfort, I would give him a method to turn that into comfort. Another person may be feeling very hopeless. I would say something to help him overcome despair.

In the evening talk my attitude is usually somewhat different than it is during the rest of the retreat. Generally, I present people a rather stern face. I treat them sternly and seriously. But during the evening talk I take a very relaxed stance and treat people in a very harmonious kind of way. This is to give people a feeling of intimacy, so that each word seems directed to them personally. This makes them more receptive to any kind of clues or encouraging advice I'm giving them. The other times when I'm very serious and strict, they may have some doubt, feeling that maybe this master is a bit insensitive, that he's pushing too hard. But after the evening talk, their attitude may change to the feeling that, well, this person does seem to have compassion and is very concerned about me. This helps to re-establish their confidence in me.

LH: I'd like to say of my experience that the things Shih-fu says at any given time in the retreat do have marvelous effects. It happened in my mind a couple of times. One time he said something at lunch that had to do with his grandmaster asking certain questions. Coming away from that meal, I had a sense of karmic connection with his grandmaster. And something really opened up for me in the afternoon. Another time Shih-fu told me, in his Chinese form of English, which is very direct and effective, that I consider that there's something very important to me inside a little box, that I was holding the box, but I had to continually turn the box one way and another to figure out how to open it. And those were just words, but when I went back to meditation I suddenly discovered that I was really actually having that experience, and it lifted my practice up onto another level.

I can attest that Shih-fu's words do have this quality of not just being words, but actually kindling, which brings about new levels of experience. It is also possibly true that Shih-fu's wishes for the people on retreat, his very pure Dharma wishes, without words, his concern and aspiration, have a direct impact on people. And this probably goes beyond being an expert retreat guide, and has something to do with a real transcendental connection that Shih-fu feels with people. There's really nothing that can be said about that — it's a kind of mystery and it's one of the deeper dimensions of what's going on in these retreats.

Shih-fu often describes four different conditions of mind — "scattered mind," "Simple mind," "one mind," and "no mind." Can you very briefly say what each one of these is?

Shih-fu: When people have just started meditation, or before they have practiced meditation, generally their mind is scattered. When a person has a lot of desires, or a lot of disappointment, or is worried about something, under those conditions, his mind is very scattered.

LH: What happens in "simple mind?"

Shih-fu: The state of "simple mind," or having relatively fewer thoughts, is when the person is beginning to work well, and their mind stays with the method almost constantly. If he should have some wandering thoughts, he immediately becomes aware of it and brings his mind back to the method, again and again.

LH: The method, by the way, might be anything from counting one's breath, or watching one's breath, to asking the question "Who am I?" or "Where am I?" But can you tell a change in a person's appearance when they're in a state of "simple mind?"

Shih-fu: Yes, I can tell. At that point the person's body will not be moving around anymore. It will be very still and his breathing will be very even, very calm. Also, when I walk behind the person, or right around the area where that person is sitting, I pick up a feeling from the person that his mind is no longer scattered.

LH: The state of "no mind" may be frightening to some people. Shih-fu gave the example of one of his students in Taiwan having the experience of "one mind" to the extent that he just felt a total identity with the whole universe. He was embracing a dog on the street, and Shih-fu came up to him and said,

"What are you doing embracing this dog?" The student said, "It's just me!" And Shih-fu struck him suddenly and said, "What! You mean you still have a 'me' there?" In other words, he was trying to lift him out of his intoxication with "one mind" into the complete clarity of "no mind," where there is no "me," no matter how big it is. Even if your "me" is as big as the whole universe, you still haven't reached the state of "no mind." You explained that there's really nothing to say about "no mind." But can you give us some indication of at least what "no mind" is not?

Shih-fu: In the state of "no mind" there is no me, no you, there is no environment. But everything is there in front of you. It's just that the mind is not moving. You perceive everything as it is, but your subjective self is not imposed on that. Your mind is totally still, but it doesn't mean there is nothing there. The people you see are still people; animals are still animals. There's no emotional reaction to things. And there's no discrimination. If a person says that they're experiencing everything as myself or that I am everything, that is not the stage of "no mind."

LH: Shih-fu, you mentioned to me in the retreat that I had enough confidence in you and that's a very important factor, the confidence in the master. I had confidence in the Three Jewels, the transcendental power of truth. But you said that I did not have strong enough confidence in myself. But what kind of self-confidence are you talking about if one is trying not to have the self? If one is practicing to drop one's self?

Shih-fu: As far as confidence, or faith, is concerned, before the person has reached the state of "no mind," when they are starting from the scattered state of mind, you must start out with "self," get a firm grasp on yourself. The "small" self should become complete and firm. This amounts to being able to concentrate the mind well. When the mind is well concentrated, the person becomes very confident. You could say their "self" is concentrated. With that kind of concentrative power of self, a strong confidence arises in your ability to go forward, to pass through the "expanded" self, or "one mind," and finally to shatter this state and reach the level of "no mind," or no-self. But when the state of "no-self" is reached, the question of faith or confidence no longer arises. It is totally irrelevant at that point.

APPENDICES

APPENDICES

Glossary

AMITABHA BUDDHA
The Buddha of the Western Paradise of the Pure Land sect. See "PURE LAND."

AMITABHA SUTRA
The principle scripture on which the Pure Land sect is based. See "PURE LAND."

ARHAT
("Noble one") In Buddhist tradition, especially Theravadin, the Arhat has completed the course of Buddhist practice, and has attained full liberation, or Nirvana. As such the Arhat is no longer subject to rebirth and death. The Mahayana tradition regards the Arhat as a less than perfect ideal, in comparison to that of the Bodhisattva who vows to postpone his own liberation until all sentient beings are delivered. See "BODHI-SATTVA."

AVATAMSAKA SUTRA
A massive Mahayana Buddhist Sutra translated from Sanskrit into Chinese in the fifth century,

seventh century, and early ninth century. The Sutra became quite popular among Chinese Buddhists and eventually became the basis of the Hua-yen philosophical school. The Ch'an school has always held it in especially high regard.

BHIKSU, BHIKSUNI

Fully ordained Buddhist monk and nun respectively.

BODHI-MIND

(Sanskrit: *bodhicitta*, "mind of awakening") In the Mahayana tradition, the aspiration for enlightenment in behalf of all sentient beings. Giving rise to the Bodhi-mind is the first step in establishing oneself on the Bodhisattva path.

BODHISATTVA

The role model in the Mahayana tradition. The Bodhisattva is a being who vows to remain in the world life after life, postponing his own full liberation until all other living beings are delivered.

BUDDHA DHARMA

The truths and teaching of Buddhism; the Dharma as taught by the Buddha. See "DHARMA."

CH'AN

(Japanese: *zen*) The Chinese transliteration of the Sanskrit word *dhyana*. Generally, the term refers to the cultivation or experience of meditative states as means for attaining enlightenment. Specifically, the term refers to the school of Chinese Buddhism known as Ch'an. In this context Ch'an also refers to the direct experience of *prajna*, or insight. Being within the Mahayana tradition, the Ch'an school, while emphasizing meditation, took the Bodhisattva ideal as the realization of Buddhist practice. In Japan, the practice and school became known as Zen.

DHARMA

Dharma has two basic meanings. On the one hand, it means the Buddhist "Law" or "Teaching." On the other hand, dharma simply refers to a thing or object, a physical or mental phenomenon. See "THREE JEWELS."

DHYANA

A Sanskrit term designating certain states of meditative absorption cultivated by Buddhist practitioners as a technique for attaining enlightenment. See "CH'AN."

DIAMOND SUTRA

(sanskrit: *Vajracchedika Sutra*) A sutra belonging to the *Prajnaparamita* (Perfection of Wisdom) system of literature, which expounds on the ultimate truth of emptiness. With the Heart Sutra, it is one of the most important scriptures in the Ch'an (and Zen) schools.

HINAYANA

The "lesser vehicle" of the *sravakas* (hearers of Buddha's teaching) and *Arhats* who strive mainly for their own personal liberation. In contrast, Mahayana, or the "great vehicle," is the broader teaching of the Bodhisattva who, out of compassion, puts his own salvation last and uses all available means to save sentient beings. (Hinayana is sometimes used to refer to Theravada, the form of Buddhism practiced in Southeast Asian countries.)

HUA-T'OU

(Japanese: *wato*) Literally, the source of words (before they are uttered), a method used in the Ch'an school to arouse the doubt sensation. The practitioner meditates on such baffling questions as: "What is *Wu*?" "Where am I?" or "Who is reciting the Buddha's name?" He does not rely on experience, logic, or reasoning. Often, these phrases are taken from kung-ans, at other times, they are spontaneously generated by the practitioner. The term "hua-t'ou" is often used interchangeably with "kung-an." See "KUNG-AN."

INCENSE BOARD/STAFF

(Chinese: *hsiang-pan*; Japanese: *kyosaku*) A long, flat board used in the meditation hall to tap dozing practitioners or to help provide the final impetus to realization for those who are "ripe." Not to be confused with "INCENSE STICK."

INCENSE STICK

One sitting period; the time it takes for one stick of incense to burn down, approximately thirty minutes. Not to be confused with "INCENSE BOARD/STAFF."

KARMA

Basically, the law of cause and effect to which all sentient beings, indeed, all things, are subject. Also, the cumulative causal situation affecting one's destiny as a result of past acts, thoughts, emotions.

KARMIC AFFINITY

A bond or connection between people due to a relationship (either good or bad) formed in a previous life. Frequently such an affinity is discussed in terms of "causes and conditions." Cause focuses on the specific karmic disposition of the individual; conditions refer to the nexus of causes that make up his situation.

KARMIC OBSTRUCTIONS

Hindrances to one's practice or life arising specifically as a result of deeds performed in this life or in past lives.

KSITIGARBHARAJA

(Chinese: *Ti-tsang*, "earth store") Bodhisattva known for his great vows to liberate all sentient beings, even to the point of descending into the hell realm in order to lead the beings there out of suffering.

KUAN YIN

(Sanskrit: *Avalokitesvara*, "the lord who looks down") Literally, "he/she who observes the sounds," the Great Bodhisattva of compassion who hears and responds to the cries of all living beings. Avalokitesvara can be both male and female. Though in China, the compassionate Bodhisattva is usually depicted in the female form, Kuan Yin.

KUNG-AN

(Japanese: *koan*) Literally, a "public case," as in a law case. Ch'an method of meditation in which the practitioner energetically and single-mindedly pursues the answer to an enigmatic question posed by his master, or which arises spontaneously. The question can only be answered by abandoning logic and reasoning, and by intuitively resolving the "doubt sensation" which gave rise to the question. Famous kung-an encounters were recorded and used by masters to test their disciples' understanding, or to arouse in them the enlightenment experience. The term "kung-an" is often used interchangeably with "hua-t'ou." See "HUA T'OU."

LOTUS SUTRA

(Sanskrit: *Saddharmapundarika Sutra*, "the Sutra of the Lotus of the True Dharma") One of the earliest and most influential scriptures in the Mahayana, translated six times into Chinese between 255-601 A.D., the Lotus Sutra describes the Bodhisattva ideal, and holds that the perfect vehicle to ultimate liberation is the Great Vehicle, the Mahayana. See "ARHAT," "BODDHISATTVA," "HINAYANA."

MILAREPA

Great eleventh-century Tibetan Buddhist yogi, poet, and saint, noted for his poetry, collected as "The Hundred Thousand Songs of Milarepa." To eradicate Milarepa's bad karma, his guru, Marpa, ordered him repeatedly to build a house single-handedly, and then tear it down again and again.

PLATFORM SUTRA OF THE SIXTH PATRIARCH

A scripture attributed to the seventh-century Ch'an master, Hui-Neng. Hui-Neng was the Sixth Patriarch in the Ch'an school, and perhaps the most famous of Chinese patriarchs.

PURE LAND

(Sanskrit: *Sukhavati*) The land of Supreme Bliss, or the Western Paradise of Amitabha Buddha. It is a pure realm perfected by the power of Amitabha Buddha's vow to save living beings. Through

Amitabha's grace, any person who sincerely invokes his name and expresses the wish to be born there will be reborn in the Pure Land. See "AMITABHA BUDDHA."

SAKYAMUNI

The historical Buddha who lived in northern India during the sixth century, B.C. Son of a provincial king, he renounced the royal life, practiced austerities in the forest for six years, and finally attained Supreme Enlightenment. The rest of his life was spent wandering and teaching, thereby laying the foundations of Buddhism.

SAMADHI

Like *dhyana*, samadhi also refers to states of meditative absorption, but is a broader and more generic term than *dhyana*. Although numerous specific samadhis are mentioned in Buddhist scriptures, the term "samadhi" itself is flexible and not as specific as *dhyana*. In this book it refers to the state of "one mind," or expanded sense of self — a unity of mind and body, self and environment.

SANSKRIT

The classic Indian literary language in which the major Mahayana Buddhist scriptures are written.

SHIH-FU

(Chinese "teacher-father") A term of respect used

by a disciple when referring to or addressing his master.

SRAMANERA, SRAMANERIKA
Novice Buddhist monk and nun respectively.

SUTRAS
Generally, scriptures. Specifically, the recorded teachings of the Buddha. The distinctive mark of a Buddhist sutra is the opening line, "Thus have I heard." This indicates that what follows are the direct teachings of Buddha, as remembered and recorded by his disciples.

TAN-T'IEN
Watching the *tan-t'ien* is a method of meditation in which one fixes one's attention on an imaginary point three finger-widths below the navel. This method has a stabilizing and centering effect, and can lead to the state of "one mind."

THREE JEWELS
Collective term referring to the Buddha, the Dharma, and the Sangha. Buddha refers to the historical founder of Buddhism, Sakyamuni. Dharma is the truth realized by the Buddha, transmitted in the scriptures, and through a lineage of enlightened masters. Sangha is the Buddhist community, originally Sakyamuni Buddha's immediate disciples. In a limited sense it consists

of Buddhist monks, nuns, and disciples; in a broader sense it includes all persons connected through belief in and practice of Buddhism. "Taking refuge" in the Three Jewels confirms one as a Buddhist practitioner. Faith in the Three Jewels is the recognition that Buddha, Dharma, and Sangha are all contained within all sentient beings.

UPASAKA, UPASIKA

Buddhist lay disciple (male and female respectively).

VEXATIONS

(Sanskrit: *klesa*) Attitudes, views, emotional states, or conditions, arising from attachments, that cause suffering or disharmony. More specifically, mental or physical states that hinder spiritual development and realization of enlightenment. As such, vexations include pleasant as well as unpleasant states.

VINAYA

The collection of prohibitions and ethical prescriptions, along with their explanations, that define the code of discipline for Buddhist monks and nuns.

Ch'an Retreat
Daily Schedule

4:00 am	Morning Boards *(Wake Up)*
4:15	Yoga Exercise
4:35	Meditation
6:00	Morning Service *(Chanting)*
6:20	Breakfast
6:40	Work and Rest Period *(Meditation Optional)*
8:00	Preparation for Meditation
8:20	Meditation
12:00 noon	Lunch
12:20 pm	Work and Rest Period *(Meditation Optional)*
1:00	Preparation for Meditation
1:20	Meditation
5:00	Evening Service *(Chanting)*
5:30	Supper
6:00	Rest Period *(Meditation Optional)*
6:50	Preparation for Dharma Lecture
7:00	Dharma Lecture
8:00	Meditation
10:00	Bedtime *(Meditation Optional)*

Other books by Ch'an Master Sheng-yen

THE POETRY OF ENLIGHTENMENT: POEMS BY ANCIENT CH'AN MASTERS

Translated and edited by Master Sheng-yen

A collection of ten poems which flow directly from the minds of enlightened Ch'an masters, communicating the nature of realization, as well as how to practice, the attitudes to cultivate, and the dangers to beware. Anyone interested in the traditional development and the essence of the teaching of Ch'an will find a wealth of information in this book. (Price: $5.95)

FAITH IN MIND: A GUIDE TO CH'AN PRACTICE

By Master Sheng-yen

A guide to Ch'an practice based upon the famous poem attributed to the seventh century Ch'an Master Seng Ts'an. During Ch'an retreats spanning several years, Master Sheng-yen commented on this work in the context of daily meditation practice; therefore, it is a day by day chronicle of the problems that arise during meditation and their resolutions. (Price: $6.95)

OX HERDING AT MORGAN'S BAY

By Master Sheng-yen

A series of practice-oriented informal talks on the Ten Ox Herding Pictures which have been used since the seventh Century to help explain the process of Ch'an practice. The pictures are familiar, but Master Sheng-yen has applied fresh insights to the images as he relates them to the actual struggles and obstacles of Ch'an practice. (Price: $3.95)

Available from Dharma Drum Publishing:
Institute of Chung-Hwa Buddhist Culture
90-56 Corona Ave., Elmhurst, NY 11373